Praise for *What Your Money Means*

"Frank Hanna has written an impressive and important book based on careful research and his own personal journey. There is a rich literature available on philanthropy in America, but I am not aware of another text that provides such **useful guidance on the central issues of both how much wealth is enough and how wealth can best be given to worthy causes.** This book should be read by potential givers both large and small."—Charles B. Knapp, President Emeritus, The University of Georgia

"Many people think about how great it would be to have a lot of money, and how they would help others or support worthy causes if they did. However, those who have attained some measure of wealth usually quickly discover that giving the money away well is often more difficult than it was to make it. Venture capitalist Frank Hanna III has thought hard about what makes philanthropy effective, and in *What Your Money Means*, he proposes some useful rules for not only how one might give away money, but as the title says, what that money means. **I highly recommend this book to everyone who plans to engage in charitable giving—no matter how much money they may have to give.**"—Thomas S. Monaghan, Founder, Ave Maria University and Founder of Domino's Pizza

"Frank Hanna digs through centuries of wise thought from Socrates, Plato, and Tacitus to Henry Ford and P O'Rourke to crystallize an intelligent approach to allocating and enjoying wealth. Smile-provoking cartoons on almost every other page make his erudite discussion fun. The journey through his book edifies those with lots of wealth—or little. **No one should give away a cent without reading this book first.**"—Foster Friess, Founder of Brandywine Funds

"In 2005, Federal Reserve data showed that the average American adult owed $1.18 for every dollar of his or her disposable income.

Translation: Americans have a problem with money—understanding it, stewarding it, and using it for their own real happiness and the happiness of others. Frank Hanna is no stranger to financial achievement. His record of support for good causes is extraordinary. **But what makes his book unique is its simple clarity, engaging style and practical value for every reader, whether wealthy or more modest of means.** This is a wonderful book of wisdom and encouragement—encouragement to use the resources God gives us for a greater purpose and our own deeper happiness, and not be used or owned by them."—Charles J. Chaput, O.F.M. Cap., Archbishop of Denver

"The world could use more Good Samaritans. Frank Hanna shows you how to become one. In this practical and thought-provoking book, a man who has truly put his money where his heart is leads others to appreciate the hidden value of wealth and how it can be used to promote the common good. Who knew giving away money could be such a good investment? **No businessperson should miss this one.** Frank Hanna's book will save you assets, time, and quite possibly your soul." Raymond Arroyo, Author of the *New York Times* bestseller *Mother Angelica* and EWTN News Director

"My experiences with wealthy people have taught me that few donors connect the meaning of their lives to the charitable causes they support. Whether it is one's faith or life philosophy that inspires personal philanthropy, this book appeals to any person serious about tithing and sharing. Frank provides simple, easy-to-follow advice on how to donate with decisiveness and **get the most bang for your charitable buck.**"—Jim Towey, President, Saint Vincent College

WHAT
YOUR
MONEY
MEANS

WHAT YOUR MONEY MEANS

(AND HOW TO USE IT WELL)

FRANK J. HANNA III

A Crossroad Book
The Crossroad Publishing Company
New York

The Crossroad Publishing Company
16 Penn Plaza, Suite 1550, New York, NY 10001
Copyright © 2008 by Frank Hanna

Printed in the United States of America

Library of Congress Cataloging-in-Publication Data on file

ISBN 10 0-8245-2520-5
ISBN 13 978-0-8245-2520-0

1 2 3 4 5 6 7 8 9 10 11 12   14 13 12 11 10 09 08

contents

foreword

I have been fortunate in life, and have received many blessings. In 1995, I found myself with a measure of financial success greater than what I had anticipated.

When I was in my second year of college, I was sitting in one of my finance classes, and I came upon an idea that I thought might make some money. I ran the idea past my father, who was in a related business, and while he told me my theory made some sense, he did not have the time or resources to pursue it.

That was 1982. As with many things in life, the right timing is crucial, and the timing for my idea in 1982 was not right. But in 1989, after seven years of keeping my eyes and ears open for the right timing and the right opportunity, it came along. My brother and I started the business and six years later sold it to a New York private equity firm for enough money that we would never have to work again. Hooray! Hip Hip Hooray!

I was thrilled. My father had raised my brother and me to be successes in business, and now we were. I was 33 and my brother was 31. But now what?

What were we to do with that money and with our lives? I have always liked what Socrates said about the unexamined life—that it was not worth living—and so I resolved that I would not spend my money and my energy and my time in an unexamined manner. But that meant I would have to spend a lot of time examining—money, my own life with money, and the lives and thoughts of others who had dealt with the concept of money.

This book is the result of that examination. I originally just gathered notes for myself. Soon, I realized that I needed to organize my thoughts and notes to be able to have something of a paradigm through which I could understand what I had gathered. And as I pulled it all together, I realized that my brother might also benefit from reading it. After he read it, I shared it with some friends, some of whom had a lot of money and some of whom had to struggle with their financial survival every day, and both groups of friends seemed to benefit from it.

In the end, money is an integral part of the world in which we live, and the failure to think about it clearly can easily lead to hazardous results. Conversely, the proper understanding and use of money can help us lead far more fulfilling lives than we might otherwise expect. In fact, a better understanding of our money can even help us achieve a richer and deeper appreciation of those things that money can't buy.

Along those lines, I am grateful to all those who have taught me of such things: my beloved wife Sally, my daughter Elizabeth, my parents, my grandparents, my brother and sister, and all those others in my life who paused to share their wisdom with me. In particular, I am indebted to a number of friends who helped me to develop the ideas for this book, rewrite what needed rewriting, edit what needed editing, and generally formulate the presentation better than I could have on my own. Among them are my wife and daughter, my father Frank, brother David, Pat Cipollone, Rob Arkley, John Barger, Ann Corkery, Deal Hudson, James Kelly, and James Larson. Elizabeth was also of great help in picking out the cartoons! I cannot repay the debt I owe to them, but I can be grateful to them, which I am.

PART 1

WHAT YOUR
MONEY MEANS

chapter 1

money demands
answers

We are tested by Wealth,
as gold is tested by fire.
—Chinese proverb

WE SPEND YEARS LEARNING HOW TO MAKE MONEY, BUT WE NEVER EXPECT THAT SPENDING IT—IN PARTICULAR, SPENDING IT WISELY—WILL BE SO CHALLENGING . . . OR SO FRUSTRATING.

Yet sometimes it's almost impossible to decide which of the countless good things that money can do we ought to be trying to do, and when we should begin devoting our wealth to those tasks: now or later.

It's not that we don't have plenty of people ready to tell us how and when to part with our money.

We do, and many of them want some of it.

Then there are all those other people who figure out for us how we should use it: economists, sociologists, psychologists, financial planners, and various academics and experts, almost all of whom are folks who haven't worked to accumulate wealth, and who don't really understand what it's like, day-to-day, to carry its burdens.

◆ ◆ ◆

It's a late afternoon at the office and the phone rings. It's my friend asking me to give to a charity he favors.

"Sure! I'll be happy to help. I'll send a check tomorrow."

A week later the phone rings again. This time it's another friend, and he's also got a reasonable request. I don't hesitate to promise to send money to the cause he wants me to help.

I hang up and remember F. A. Harper's remark: "Giving in many instances is really little more than the cost of peacefully evicting a well-intentioned trespasser."[1]

Did I make that last donation just to get someone off my back? Did I give enough? Was I properly motivated?

I think my motives are good.

Like you, I'm willing to share my money. You and I really do want to help the needy, and, while providing what we should for our own families, we do want to contribute to others as much as we ought to give. Some of us may even donate a great amount of money to charity.

But the casual ways we do so—a contribution here, work with a charity there—bother me more with every passing day. I didn't grow wealthy handling money haphazardly; I ought not to be giving it away haphazardly.

You and I have strict standards by which to judge the kinds of business projects we invest in; we're careful to determine whether we should get involved in those projects and how much we should invest now and later.

Shouldn't we approach the challenge of charity in the same way?

◆ ◆ ◆

I know there are many good causes out there and that my contributions can make a significant difference for many of them. But it's just not always clear what my obligations are to charity and what those obligations mean for my wealth and the way I should spend it.

As far as that goes, it's not even clear how much money is enough for me and my family. I do have more than one family can use on itself, but should I give the rest away?

If so, how much?

And when?

And how can I be sure?

Would giving substantial amounts today be good for my family, for my businesses, or even, ultimately, for the needy?

You see, I've got a knack for making money, and in twenty years I might quadruple the value of what I could give today. Should I give my wealth away today—or twenty years from now?

Maybe you and I should just stay put: devote the rest of our lives to making money—which might be what we do well—and then give it away once our earning ability ceases or we pass away. That guarantees charities the largest contribution.

Perhaps.

Most of us have families and others who depend on us—employees, stockholders, or co-workers who expect us to sustain the business from which they derive their salaries or income. Would it be morally permissible for us to walk away from them in order to serve others? Might it even be wrong for us to cease creating wealth now that could later be used to serve others?

Then there's that more radical response that some established men and women have given. With twenty or thirty good working years still ahead of them, they've stepped away from the enterprises that brought them their money and power. Are you and I called to take such a radical step? Should we stop making money today and devote the rest of our lives to using what we have now to support good causes?

Are there reasonable criteria by which we can make such judgments?

Questions, questions, questions.

"Are we spending our money as we should?"

"Are we living our lives as we should?"

◆ ◆ ◆

For a number of years I've grappled with these questions; and I've talked to enough people like you to know that you grapple with them too! Knowing the great good that my money could do—if only I knew better how and when I should employ it—and confident that these questions can be answered with as much certainty as I answer questions of business strategy, I decided a few years ago to tackle directly this problem of wealth and its obligations, and to do so with the same rigor that I approach business deals. I wanted to figure out—once and for all, for myself and for people like you— just what it means for us to have money, and what we should be doing with it.

Although these pages answer questions for people who've inherited "Old Money," they're primarily aimed at hard-working men and women who are still deeply engaged in intense efforts to generate wealth: folks who have strong wills, quick minds, and a sure grasp of what it takes, day-by-day, to make money now.

If, like me, you value the virtues of capitalism and moral virtue but have too often been stymied when you've tried to figure out just what you should be doing with your money, then this book is for you.

Here I'll offer you a lean, no-nonsense explanation of the meaning of your money, and provide a guide for dealing with it constructively. Some of what I conclude won't surprise you: sometimes you'll find me formulating things that you've figured out already. (That's not a weakness. If my conclusions were contrary to your experience—you'd have reason to distrust them.) Other times you'll think my conclusions are novel.

In some respects they are, but they're not original. For when I began considering these topics seriously, I discovered an understanding of wealth that developed almost 2,500 years ago with the great philosopher Aristotle and was subsequently embraced by Cicero, St. Thomas Aquinas, Ralph Waldo Emerson, Andrew Carnegie, and a wide assortment of wise souls in other times and cultures—an understanding rooted not in religion or mysticism, but in ordinary virtue, common sense, and the pragmatism that allows societies to flourish.

In this long tradition I found clear, simple criteria you and I can use to determine how much money is enough for us, now, and in the future, too. I'm going to explain these criteria to you so that by the time you finish reading you'll have in hand a number of simple rules of thumb that will enable you to judge whether you're using your money as you ought, and will empower you to respond as carefully and as confidently to your wealth, to its demands, and to your charitable impulses as you do to business proposals.

These guidelines will provide easy ways for you to determine how much of your money you should devote to the common good, and when you should do so—now, later, or when you die. Best of all, they'll show you how to use what you keep as an instrument to strengthen your family and your relations to your loved ones, while making each of you wiser and the world a better place.

◆ ◆ ◆

Before we move on, a personal note is appropriate: when I finally decided to try to address these questions that have nagged at me for so long, I resolved to follow the evidence where it leads and not to draw back from conclusions that might leave me uncomfortable or looking bad.

In my businesses and in my private life, I've always believed that if I'm going to handle things the way they ought to be handled, I've got to do four things:

1. Find out the truth about how things are now.
2. Discover the truth about how they're supposed to be.
3. Figure out how to change things from how they are now to how they're supposed to be.
4. Make myself want to change them enough that I'll do what's necessary to bring about that change.

In my businesses and in these pages, discovering what's true is my first task. That's how this book came about; and I hope that, regarding wealth and its meaning, the ideas, principles, and guidelines I present here will help you to see the truth of how things are now and how they're supposed to be.

I've generally found that once I've accomplished the first two steps (discovering the truth of how things are and how they are supposed to be), the hard work begins. That's when I've got to figure out how to get from how they are to how they're supposed to be, and—the hardest thing of all—I've got to make myself want to make that change.

I mention these four steps because although by researching and writing this book I've largely accomplished for myself steps one and two; I'm still working on steps three and four. It's not easy for folks like you and me, accustomed as we are to a certain way of life, to examine our attitudes and habits. It's even harder to want to change them.

So although the book is done, my own life is still a work in progress.

For a number of years, as they grew clearer in my mind, I've slowly been embracing the principles enunciated in these pages and shifting the way I live so that I'm abiding more closely by these guidelines . . . but I'm not there yet.

That's why you'll sometimes find me explaining and defending standards that I don't yet live by. That's because either I see they're true but haven't yet gathered enough interior strength to make myself live by them or I'm in the process of changing from my old ways

*"I've learned to live without a lot of things, Herb,
but money isn't one of them."*

to the better ones I explain here, and I just haven't completed the transformation.

◆ ◆ ◆

So let's make a pact—about this book and about our lives. Together we'll inquire into the truth, regardless of where it leads us. Then, having seen the truth, we'll each try to live in accordance with what we've learned.

But we'll always understand that we each are works in progress, and we'll never judge each other, but rather will support each other as we try to learn the meaning of our wealth and to discover the uses that each of us, uniquely, are called to make of it.

Money demands answers. The more it grows, the more difficult the questions become. Chief among those questions is, "Am I using my money as I ought?"

Once you finish reading the following chapters, you'll be closer to answering that question, able to say (as do I): "No, not yet. But now I see more clearly what I need to do and how to go about doing it. I've got some changes to make and it's gonna take time. Come back next year. Ask me then, 'Are you spending your money as you should?'" and I'll be able to say to you with confidence, "Yes. Yes, I am. I'm healthy and wealthy; and, about money, I'm becoming wise: I'm well on the road to using it as I should."

chapter 2

the meaning of your
money and mine

Well, whiles I am a beggar, I will rail
And say there is no sin but to be rich;
And being rich, my virtue then shall be
To say there is no vice but beggary.[2]
—Shakespeare (1564–1616)

S HAKESPEARE WAS WONDERFULLY ABLE TO SHOW US HUMAN NA-
TURE AS IT IS, PARADING BEFORE US VANITY AND PRIDE, HUMILITY
AND INTEGRITY, LUST AND HYPOCRISY, AND ALL THE OTHER
VIRTUES, VICES, AND QUIRKS THAT MAKE US WHO WE ARE. IN THE PAS-
SAGE ABOVE QUOTED FROM *KING JOHN*, THE BASTARD CELEBRATES THE
MYOPIA, DELIBERATE OR NOT, OF THOSE WHO HAVE MONEY OR HAVE IT
NOT.

In this chapter, I want to provide an explanation of the meaning
of money and engage you in the thought process that led me to it.
Hearing too well the song of the Bastard in *King John,* I want to

"After my gall-bladder operation, I said to myself, 'Whoa, man,
what are you doing with your life?'
So I sold my blue chips and put it all into Treasury bills."

ensure that I don't fall unconsciously into the hypocrisy that the Bastard celebrates and so ably mocks.

For years, that's been my fear, a fear that became a major reason that I undertook the investigation of which this book is the fruit.

It's simply not right for those of us who have money to take it for granted. We've each of us got to confront the reality of our money and seek to discern its meaning, not only in our own lives but in the overall scheme of things.

Just as Socrates insisted that "the unexamined life is not worth living,"[3] so I'm convinced that unexamined wealth is not worth having. Indeed, as I will demonstrate in just a moment, it's downright dangerous—to those of us who have it and to those we love. With the stakes so high, it would be wrong of us to act like the Bastard and cavalierly defend it because we have it.

No.

Either we discover its meaning and live in accordance with that meaning, or rid ourselves of it, because, like fire, it will harm us if we don't use it as it's meant to be used and handle it as it needs to be handled.

◆ ◆ ◆

When I launched this investigation into the meaning of money, I didn't realize that these concerns of mine have occupied the minds of rich and poor for all of recorded history. Nor did I realize that there was, among the wise and from time immemorial, an unbroken understanding of the meaning of wealth—an understanding that makes as much sense today as it did when it was first enunciated thousands of years ago.

This understanding is rooted not in the accidental circumstances or desires of this or that wealthy man, wealthy nation, or wealthy generation. Nor is it a religious understanding of the meaning of money (although it's consistent with the teachings of the greatest world religions). Rather, its foundation lies in prehistory and is grounded in the nature of the universe itself.

Indeed, what I'll present to you in the next few dozen pages is simply common sense applied to questions larger than those we generally address, questions that produce a commonsense answer to the meaning of your money and mine, too.

It will take us just a few pages to get there, but the answer it affords—and the difference it made in my life and will make in yours—is well worth the time spent.

We're on the verge of the answer to the question that brushes against our cheek after we leave a sumptuous meal, the question that sits with us on long night flights, whispering doubts in our ears as we stare down at the landscape five miles below us.

"Are we spending our money as we ought?"

The Bounty of the Earth Is for All Men and Women

As heaven is for the gods, so the earth has been given to all mankind, and lands uninhabited are common to all.[4]

Tacitus (c. 55—c. 117)

The wonderful thing about our world is that the *essentials* we each need to survive are, in principle at least, available to each of us: food, water, shelter.[5] I don't mean that each of us actually and always has access to these *essentials*. With poverty so great in our world, that's patently false.

I mean that we weren't put into a forbidding world like Mars which produces neither food for us to eat, water to drink, or trees that can be formed into shelter. No matter how great our wealth, had we been born on Mars where none of the *essentials* exist, our physical nature would have condemned us to a quick and dusty death.

No.

You and I were put into a rich world that provides us the *essentials* that, by nature, we need a world wonderfully proportioned to our needs, a world that, in all its basics (land, air, water, weather, and the millions of plants and animals that populate it) and in its goodness and beauty, seems particularly designed to sustain us, to make us thrive, and even to give us joy.

God did not place us into this world filled with the *essentials* that by our nature we need, and then condemn us to quick death by denying us the right to use these *essentials* to sustain ourselves.

Instead, on the use of the fruits of the earth, there has been no divine prohibition or other natural prohibition that we have ever encountered.

At this fact we marvel too little. We were not just placed on this planet; the planet was given to us for our home.

Given.

We did not purchase it; we did not inherit it.

It was given.

And not only the planet, but the universe itself.

About this astounding fact, MIT astrophysicist Alan Guth commented, "It's said that there's no such thing as a free lunch. But the universe is the ultimate free lunch."[6]

The earth, too, and the things in it are a free lunch. The first men and women ever to enter a land years ago found there cold streams from which to drink, apples and pears to eat, deer, rabbits, and pheasants to hunt, and fish to catch. These first humans drank freely of the waters they found, ate the fruits of the trees, hunted the game, and caught the fish.

In that land, and in every other uninhabited place they first went to, the bounty of the earth was freely set before them. It was fitting and right for those men and women to use that bounty to provide themselves the *essentials* they needed to live and thrive. As philosopher John Stuart Mill pointed out, "No man made the land. It is the original inheritance of the whole species. Its appropriation is wholly a question of general expediency."[7]

Nor is there any reason to think the *essentials* were set there only for that group or any other specific group. Those people were able to use those particular goods of the earth only for as long as they themselves lived—or lived in that valley—and if, as often happened in times long past, that group moved on to other valleys, there's no reason to conclude that their sojourn there, whether long or short, somehow denied its use to others who might come after them.

Would a new group arriving in that uninhabited valley have less right to its fruits than the first group that had arrived and left hundreds of years before?

No.

That's why thousands of generations of souls across the world have been free to drink deeply of the waters of our blessed and bountiful planet, eat the fruit of its trees, warm themselves by the heat of its fires, use the wood of its forests to cook the food they catch or gather, and light their nights under the dome of the beautiful stars.

Generations of Christians have acknowledged this perennially renewed, unasked for, and unmerited bounty of creation in the simple grace many of them still say before meals: "Bless us, O Lord, and these Thy gifts, which we are about to receive from Thy bounty"— a bounty received even by those who may not be able to discern that it comes from God, a bounty received by them and their forefathers, by us and our forefathers, and by all souls who have come before us and who will come after us, a bounty suited for the well-being of humans from time immemorial, a bounty intended for just that purpose.

I don't find anything accidental in the reality of this bounty. The goods of the earth are not merely available to those who chance upon them; they've been placed here to provide the *essentials* to all men and women who have lived or who ever will live. As one wise writer puts it,

> Nothing in subhuman creation ever comes to be with a label saying: this good is meant for this person but not that one, this group but not that, people of this sort but not of that sort. Instead, both in the beginning and now, God provides all the riches of the material world for all people to use as he directs.[8]

In other words, the goods of the earth have not merely *existence*, but a *purpose*, a specific destination they're intended to reach: every living person who needs them for his or her well-being.[9] There is no person to whom they are, by nature, denied; there is no person who, in principle, lacks the right to use the goods of the earth for his or her well-being. *The goods of the earth have a universal destination:* they are meant for each and every one of us.

When we judge that they are ours alone to do with as we please, we are like the banker who gets so used to having in his bank the money of a wealthy depositor that the money almost seems like his own, not the depositor's.

When a banker starts thinking he owns the money in his vaults, the real owners of that money have problems; when you and I start thinking that, simply and absolutely, we own the goods of the earth that have been placed under our care, then the poor and the needy have problems. The goods of the earth have been given to all mankind, not just to you and me.

With regard to property, our situation is much like that of the managers of corporations. Shareholders place their assets in the hands of managers. They give those managers great latitude in deciding how to handle the assets. They pay those managers well for their services and for the expenses they incur in managing the assets.

Not for an instant, however, do the shareholders cease to own the assets, and good managers keep this fact foremost in their minds as they manage those assets. From beginning to end, the assets belong to the shareholders!

Similarly, with regard to the goods of the earth, you and I are only managers. Yes, in accordance with standards we'll enunciate later, we can keep for ourselves some of the income generated by our management of the goods of the earth, but not for an instant do we come to own the goods of the earth simply and for ourselves alone. No matter how much wealth may come to be ours, we never become more than stewards of those goods that have been placed, for the time being, in our hands to help bring about the universal destination of goods.[10]

This is a radical concept.

Even though it follows simply and directly from the nature of property and ownership, it is radical and unsettling. So unsettling that, when Jesus told the young man who was attached to his wealth that he should sell all that he had and give it to the poor, the young man walked away dejected, for he could not accept that prospect.[11] He was a manager who had come to believe that he owned the assets.

If God gave the fruits of the earth to all of mankind to provide the *essentials* for all and did not initially give any designated part of the earth or its goods to anyone in particular, why then do we so easily think that property is ours?

How did private ownership of property arise?

And what makes ownership legitimate?

Ownership Is the Prudential Division of Property into Yours and Mine

Property should be private, but the use of it common; and the special business of the legislator is to create in men this benevolent disposition.[12]

Aristotle (384–322 B.C.)

If God gave the fruits of the earth to all of mankind to provide the *essentials* for all and did not initially give any designated part of the earth or its goods to anyone in particular, how, then, did private ownership of property arise, and how can it be justified?

Almost all human societies allow private ownership of property—and the best of them promote and protect it, but since classical times the wisest of men have agreed with Cicero that "private ownership does not derive from nature."[13] Rather, from time immemorial all successful societies have adopted it because experience showed that private ownership is generally the best way to draw forth from the earth the maximum benefit for the most people. In the thirteenth century, St. Thomas Aquinas explained why it works so well, listing three ways in which private ownership yields a society that is ultimately wealthier, ordered better, and more harmonious than one which doesn't allow private ownership.[14]

Aquinas notes first that because people tend to take better care of their own property than they do of community property, private ownership makes for better care of all property. Second, when some of the goods of the earth are clearly designated mine and others are designated yours, and these divisions are publicly recognized by law or some other means, there tend to be fewer disputes within society;

communities are more harmonious. Finally, if I know that I will own (and thereby be able to use and enjoy) the fruits of my labor without the undue influence of others, I will likely work harder to draw from my property the good things it can yield. For these three reasons, Aquinas argues, smart societies promote and protect ownership of private property.

So although private ownership generally does allow me, if I choose, to keep my goods from you and you to keep yours from me, selfishness is not the primary justification for it. The strongest justification for it lies deeper, and has consequences more profound:

> *Private ownership promotes a wealthier and more*
> *harmonious society by creating incentives for owners to*
> *treat their goods better and to bring forth from them*
> *greater wealth than there would otherwise be.*

Aquinas's eight-centuries-old explanation finds confirmation in the conclusions of many modern economists that the continuing impoverishment of large areas of the world is not due to lack of sufficient natural resources or lack of a proper work ethic in impoverished peoples. Rather, hundreds of millions of people live in countries wherein it's difficult or even impossible to establish legal title to land or other significant goods, or where the government will not defend legal ownership against those who infringe on it.

Because they live in countries that don't safeguard ownership against predators, hundreds of millions of souls in underdeveloped countries lack the incentives for enterprise and development that Aquinas listed—incentives that, in countries that protect private property, have led to the creation of vast amounts of wealth by individuals assured that they'll be the ones to benefit from their efforts to create that wealth from the things they own.

That's the benefit of private property that's overlooked by so many who denounce it as selfish and seek to abolish it in favor of the poor: by dividing goods into yours and mine and giving me dominion over my property and you dominion over yours, ownership of private property brings forth benefits for everyone in society, benefits that would not be realized were there no ownership whatsoever or were all property held in common.

By ensuring that there are more goods all around and that those goods are better taken care of, private ownership promotes the creation of wealth throughout society, and on all levels of society, improving the lot of all.

Furthermore, as Aristotle noted so long ago, "There is the greatest pleasure in doing a kindness or service to friends or guests or companions, which can only be rendered when a man has private property."[15]

Without something of our own to give, we cannot give.

For prudential reasons such as these, which ultimately bring greater good from property than would abolition of ownership or communal ownership, most societies have allowed and even promoted private ownership.

◆ ◆ ◆

According to Aquinas, since private ownership of property arises from man's law not from natural law (or, if you prefer, "not from the nature of things"), there are circumstances in which God's gift of the goods of the earth to all souls takes precedence over the division of those goods into yours and mine.

The right of the government to levy taxes and the legal principle of eminent domain each are rooted in this understanding of the nature of property and the priority of the welfare of all over the property rights of individuals. Ownership is not an absolute right, but is subordinated to the universal destination of goods:

> *When property rights stand in the way of serious needs*
> *of the larger society, the government can nullify property rights.*

For the good of all, the government sometimes takes that which is the property of one or some—in the case of taxes, the government takes money, and in the case of eminent domain, it takes land or buildings.

These are just two commonly accepted consequences of the notion that private ownership must not gravely interfere with the universal destination of goods.

Because of the dangers of governmental tyranny and the risk that law might be used by some to deprive others of the rightful use of their private property, societies generally retain strict limits on the use of legal mechanisms to take money, buildings, land, or other property from individuals. Eminent domain, in particular, ought never to be used casually, and there are surely many cases in which we might think an owner ought to yield his property to the state for common good, but also think it would be wrong—and a bad precedent—for the government to seize that property.

Morally speaking, however, our obligations to use our property for the well-being of others are not so circumscribed. Legal ownership does give us the right and obligation to care for our property and wealth, and to distribute them as we choose. Morally speaking, however,

My wealth is not meant merely for myself,
nor is yours meant solely for you.

On this fundamental truth, this whole book is built.

On this same strong foundation, I believe, my life should be built.

And so should yours.

For me (and likely for many good-willed folks who have money), arriving at this conclusion has been the easiest part. I've found it much harder to determine just what this truth means for me at this time in my life, while I'm still actively involved in creating and growing a number of businesses.

Granting that my wealth is not meant merely for me and for those I love, just who is it meant for? How should I get it to them?

I don't have it lying around in cash. It's tied up in my businesses and investments. Must I dismantle my businesses, give the proceeds away, and live like Mother Teresa? Can't I just will it to charity when I die? If not, what must I do today, and how should I do it?

chapter 3

how much is enough?

If you can actually count your money
then you are not really a rich man.[16]
—J. Paul Getty (1892–1976)

THE ODDS ARE YOU'VE GOT LOTS OF OBLIGATIONS: PEOPLE WHO DEPEND ON YOU FOR FOOD, SHELTER, CLOTHING, AND MORE, AND CAN BE EXPECTED TO DEPEND ON YOU THIS WAY FOR MANY MORE YEARS. AND YOU'VE GOT TO TAKE CARE OF THE OBLIGATIONS THAT ARE UNIQUELY YOURS BEFORE YOU CONSIDER USING WHAT'S LEFT OVER TO SERVE OTHERS BEYOND YOUR DEPENDENTS.

So can you spare any of it?

Even with lots of money in the bank right now, that's not an easy question to answer. In our lifetimes you and I have seen the rise and fall of the Internet companies that drew to themselves vast amounts of capital and seemed to be rewriting the way business gets done and money made—only to crash. After a rapid accumulation of wealth, many saw that same wealth vanish.

23

Oil prices are volatile; war and terrorism have rendered chancy even businesses that once were sure things.

Can you spare any of your money?

To answer that question with confidence, you've got to determine just how far your own obligations extend and whether you have enough money to cover them—today, tomorrow, and ten (or perhaps even twenty) years from tomorrow . . . and that's not easy.

Unfortunately, you can't simply rely on an actuarial table that tells how much money is enough for the average person your age; you've got to figure out how much is enough for you in your own particular circumstances.

Only after you determine how much money is enough for you do you have to address the question of what to do with what's left over—if any is left over.

So let's develop some standards by which to judge our own financial situation. If we discover we have funds that are not already obligated for the care of our family and those close to us, then we'll try to determine whether others may have a claim to those funds.

In the process, we'll develop guidelines that will cut right through the tangle of details and obligations that each of our lives consist in, guidelines that will enable you and me to determine, in our own particular circumstances, the best things to do with the money that we have.

Bare Necessities

> *Those who have some means think that the most important thing in the world is love. The poor know that it is money.*[17]
>
> Gerald Brenan (1894–1987)

So how much money do you and I really need?

Do we only need enough for food and shelter, and clean clothes and a car to drive to work? Or do our needs extend as far as a Har-

"Would you like to see my pile?"

vard education for our children? For you and for me, how much is enough?

When I began studying this problem, I found answers that careen from one extreme to the other. To the Bible's familiar warning that "The love of money is the root of all evil,"[18] the ever flippant Mark Twain counters, "The lack of money is the root of all evil."[19] But it was author John Updike, who, speaking about another topic, gave the estimate of money that seems accepted by most people these days: "Sex is like money, only too much is enough."[20]

Encountering so many and such strong opinions, I realized I was dealing with one of those large topics, which, like mountains, are seen best by starting far from them. When it comes to money, *enough* is such a concept. So let's begin by considering people who are far from wealthy; let's start with destitute people who clearly don't have enough.

Mother Teresa of Calcutta (1910–1997) devoted forty years of her life to those people she called "the poorest of the poor," the destitute and dying souls found living on the dusty streets of the city, people who spend their days begging and their nights sleeping in doorways. Wasted by malnutrition and disease, these people lack money even for the *bare necessities* that keep us alive: food, water, shelter, and minimal medical care.

The plight of the desperately poor gives us the first and most obvious piece in the puzzle of money we hope to solve:

A person who can't afford the bare necessities doesn't have enough money.[21]

What about you and me?

Do we have enough for the *bare necessities?* Not just for ourselves, but for all those who depend on us? That's not hard to answer.

Bare Necessities
To find out how much money is enough for our *bare necessities,* we have to ask ourselves: "How much do I need just to keep myself and my dependents alive, with absolutely nothing left over?"

For us, how much money is enough? If we can't afford the *bare necessities,* we don't have enough money; and if we're spending all our money on *bare necessities,* then we're spending our money as we ought.

Later we'll see that, spiritually at least, it's permissible and good for even the destitute to reserve some small portion of what they have—the proverbial Widow's Mite—to give to others. That gift, however small, establishes and certifies as free and noble the impoverished man or woman who voluntarily makes such a sacrifice. It makes clear to themselves and others that their impoverishment is merely bodily, not spiritual.

For the moment, our question is not whether it's permissible for persons who don't have enough money for *bare necessities* to contribute to others; our question is merely whether such persons have enough.

They don't. And their admirable choice to share with others the little they have doesn't change our answer: a person who can't afford the *bare necessities* doesn't have enough money.

But after you and I pay for our *bare necessities* and the *bare necessities* of those who depend on us, we still have lots of money left over. To get to the core of the money questions you and I now face, we've got to go further.

Genuine Needs

> *Resolve not to be poor: whatever you have, spend less. Poverty is a great enemy to human happiness; it certainly destroys liberty, and it makes some virtues impracticable, and others extremely difficult.*[22]
>
> Samuel Johnson (1709–1784)

On a level above the destitute are those among us who have the *bare necessities* but not much more. They may have shelter, but it fails to protect them from winter's cold. Drafts disturb the candles that light their unheated houses. Summer brings mosquitoes and stinging flies through glassless windows and cracks in the makeshift walls.

These impoverished souls have no electricity or indoor plumbing. There's food enough to keep them alive, but it doesn't provide them the vitamins, minerals, carbohydrates, and protein they need, and they often go to bed hungry.

Author James Baldwin describes this state well: "Anybody who has ever struggled with poverty knows how extremely expensive it is to be poor."[23] Impoverished children may never go to school or may attend classes for just a few years; many never learn to read, so they spend their lives in dead-end jobs. Medical care? Perhaps the impoverished receive it in emergencies, but more than likely they don't.

Eyeglasses and dental care are out of the question. Truly, as Samuel Johnson notes, "Poverty is a great enemy to human happiness."

Impoverished souls can survive a long time without proper food, shelter, and medical care, but these are not luxuries; and when they remain unfulfilled, humans can't flourish. Indeed, even before we're born, these factors are critical. Pregnant women who are not economically able to eat a proper diet that includes the right vitamins and minerals give birth to children who don't develop as they should physically and mentally. Throughout their lives, the health of these babies is worse than average; they're more prone to learning disabilities and psychomotor problems; their mental and psychological development is often stunted in ways that can prevent them from becoming fully self-sufficient citizens. This is only part of "how extremely expensive it is to be poor."

◆ ◆ ◆

How different humans are from creatures like the wasp!

The instant a baby wasp emerges from its egg, it has all the characteristics and abilities of an adult wasp. Only size differentiates it from its parent. A baby wasp has one need alone: food. And food merely serves to keep it alive so it can grow to a larger physical size.

Human babies, in contrast, are born helpless and unformed.

Yes, genetically at least, they are formed with inherent potentials: every baby is designed to become a certain kind of being—a physically able adult, mentally alert, capable of grasping abstract concepts and making prudent, morally responsible decisions as a free and full member of society. And a child nourished properly and raised in optimal conditions will reach this nature-intended goal unless something untoward prevents him from doing so.

Therefore, to become what they're genetically intended to be, humans need years of physical, emotional, intellectual, and moral care from adults: food, warmth, shelter, medical care, education, and love.

For humans, these are not luxuries, they're *genuine needs*; and you and I have to provide them for ourselves and for those who depend on us.

Genuine needs are the things a person must have
in order to develop as he should,
physically, morally, intellectually, and spiritually.

So to *bare necessities,* we must add *genuine needs,* a second category of goods that are essential to a proper human life. It's not greed or avarice that leads a parent to want to provide for the *genuine needs* of his child.

◆ ◆ ◆

Now because nature doesn't change, the natural needs of a wasp never vary from century to century. Nor—physically, at least—do the *genuine needs* of a human being: the vitamins that today fend off rickets would have prevented it in Caesar's time, too; the statins that some of us take to prevent the buildup of cholesterol in our arteries would have kept open the arteries of Henry VIII.

Genuine needs of a physical nature remain largely the same from generation to generation and from culture to culture. Nor are they usually hard to identify: cavities won't kill an impoverished child, but no one's front teeth ought to rot out; lack of eyeglasses won't kill a woman, but she won't be able to see as she's meant to see. With more money, *genuine needs* such as these can easily be taken care of.

Unlike wasps, humans live not merely in nature but in culture, and culture varies from place to place and century to century, creating other *genuine needs* in order to thrive. Whereas, for example, five hundred years ago reading played a significant role only in the lives of a minority of souls and was needed only by that tiny percentage of them whose profession involved written materials, our world today is a writing-based culture. Today in Western culture the person who cannot read is severely limited in his ability to become an independent, responsible person capable of finding decent employment and making prudent decisions. Similarly, a farsighted man

who can't afford glasses won't be able to get or keep a job that requires him to read. In the last few centuries, the ability to read has
become a *genuine need*, albeit a genuine cultural need. In the next
twenty years, it could well be that the ability to use a computer will
become a *genuine need* worldwide, as the computer becomes one of
the primary means by which individuals engage the world, from
seeking information to purchasing goods.

When such *genuine needs*, physical and otherwise, are not satisfied, it's very difficult for us to become the persons we're meant to
become: wise and capable citizens who are called to play a full and
fruitful role in society for our own good and the good of all.

Although we can survive without them, things such as eyeglasses,
dental care, and even a basic education are not luxuries indulged in
by the privileged elite; they're *genuine needs*.

They give us a sure grasp of the second piece of our money puzzle:

A person who can't afford to pay for
his own genuine needs and the genuine needs
of his dependents doesn't have enough money.

"Feeling poorly? Thank heaven! I thought
you said you were feeling poor."

◆ ◆ ◆

Although the *bare necessities* for each of us are roughly the same, *genuine needs* can vary not only from age to age and from culture to culture, but even from person to person living at the same time in the same culture.

Let me tell you about my friend, Jack. He lives in a quiet New England town and has a job just ten minutes from his house. He spends his days managing a small firm that sells products by mail.

Jack has twelve kids, seven of whom are still at home. Twelve kids means that, in dollars alone, Jack's *bare necessities* and his *genuine needs* exceed those of my family which is much smaller; and they exceed the *bare necessities* and *genuine needs* of almost every other family man in America.

How does he spend his money?

His food bills are huge, especially with his three teenage boys. Then there are the medical expenses: even in months when they're not at the emergency room with a bad cut or broken arm, there are shots for the little ones and regular check-ups. The supplies for his diabetic child cost a lot, and so do Jack's cholesterol drugs. Plus some of the kids have bad allergies.

With seven kids still at home, there are nine of them (counting his wife and him) to keep clothed and shod. Winter boots and coats are expensive, even when they get them used. Six of them have to be kept in eyeglasses, and then there's the dentist—even though they strictly enforce tooth brushing, they wind up filling dozens of cavities each year.

But that's cheap compared to the orthodontist. Jack's kids have small jawbones so their teeth are too crowded and grow in crooked. Some have to be pulled and the others straightened. Right now they've got two kids in braces.

Add to that the hot water bill for all the showers the older kids take, the school supplies, the swimming lessons, drivers' education, and the cost of involvement in school activities and sports—Jack has to earn a hefty salary. Even so, there's no money left over.

Even if we exclude from Jack's *genuine needs* the orthodontist, drivers' ed, school sports, and other such expenses, Jack's answer to the question of "how much money is enough?" is probably "about three times or four times as much as the average American"—and that's just for *bare necessities* and his family's *genuine needs.*

So even in the same culture at the same time, *genuine needs* can vary widely, causing some people to need far more money than others. Nonetheless, although *genuine needs* of persons like Jack may differ in dollar value from yours or mine, they don't differ in kind. *Genuine needs* are largely the same within any particular culture at any particular time.

Now what about you and me?

◆ ◆ ◆

In light of what we have discovered, what are our *genuine needs?* How much money do you and I need to pay for them?

> *Genuine Needs*
>
> To find out how much is enough for our genuine needs, we have to ask ourselves: "How much does it cost to provide myself and my dependents with decent housing, adequate medical and dental care, a fundamental education, and the other basic goods we need to develop as we should physically, morally, intellectually and spiritually?"

For you and me, how much money is enough?

> *If we can't afford to pay for our own bare necessities*
> *and genuine needs and those of our dependents,*
> *we don't have enough money.*

If we're spending all our money on *bare necessities* and *genuine needs,* then we're spending our money as we ought.[24]

Profession-related Needs

Profligacy consists not in spending years of time or chests of money,—but in spending them off the line of your career.[25]

Ralph Waldo Emerson (1803–1882)

After you and I pay for our *bare necessities* and *genuine needs*, we've still got money left over. To get to the core of the money questions you and I now face, we have to expand our considerations which I will illustrate by comparison. I know of a man here in America who has a wife and just two daughters. George is proud of where he lives. It's an elegant, 200-year-old mansion with 132 rooms, 35 bathrooms, 28 fireplaces, and 3 elevators! There are 5 full-time chefs and he frequently hosts dinner parties for as many as 140 guests. He has an indoor tennis court, a heated indoor pool, exercise machines, a small movie theatre where he, his wife, and a few friends gather to watch first-run movies. There's a billiard room, and, just outside, a putting green and a jogging track he uses regularly. Every night his servants launder his clothes, press them, and return them fresh to him in the morning.

This fellow travels around town by limousine or helicopter. He loves foreign cities and frequently travels the world in a jet he keeps fueled and ready at all times, in case he chooses to go somewhere on short notice.

How much does it cost to live that way?

I don't think he watches the numbers closely, but just maintaining the mansion and entertaining his guests costs about $9 million a year!

◆ ◆ ◆

What about Jack?

He spends less than $4,500 a year to entertain and keep his house in shape: 1/2000th of the amount George spends on the very same things!

But George is not a profligate.

He's president of the United States.

The 200-year-old mansion is the White House.

His duties require him to travel frequently and far. As part of his job, he has to host large gatherings for heads of state, diplomats, politicians, businessmen, and others. He's also got to serve them food that will delight them: thus, five chefs and banquet space for 140 guests at a time.

Men under the stresses he endures require regular exercise and leisure, but security prevents him from going to the local gym for a workout or to the local theatre for a movie. Hence exercise equipment, the indoor pool, the jogging track, the movie theatre, and other in-house facilities that wouldn't be needed by someone less in need of strict security and constant access to the reins of government.

One hundred thirty-two rooms and 35 bathrooms?

You might quibble about whether that many are needed, but efficiency and security have moved much of the business of governing right into the White House, along with the large staff that that requires. Indeed, all but the most important offices in the White House are cramped even by the standards of ordinary workers.

Now it's true but irrelevant for our purposes that the president doesn't pay for any of these facilities, for the social functions he hosts in them, or for his official trips around the world. That's because, for the moment at least, we're trying to come up with criteria to determine how much money we need, not how to pay for what we need.

Before we knew that George was president, his lifestyle seemed selfish and profligate. George's profession, however, casts it in an entirely different light. His profession places demands on him far beyond those of ordinary men and women. Clearly, if we're to determine how much we have to have beyond *bare necessities* and *genuine needs*, we each have to consider what we must have in order to fulfill our profession:

Profession-related needs are those things required of us
in order to fulfill our profession in life.

◆ ◆ ◆

Now the president is unique in that most of his *profession-related needs* are automatically provided by his employer, the people of the United States for the governing of their country. The rest of us have many *profession-related needs* we have to pay for out of our own pocket.

I asked Jack about his *profession-related needs.*

"Well, unlike the president," he responded, "I can stay close to home and help my wife manage the kids and the household. I almost never go on business trips. In fact, except for an occasional trip to the beach with the kids, I rarely leave town and I haven't been out of the country for many years. Generally, I'm within five miles of my house: either at work, at home, or at church.

"At work, I do all my business by phone, fax, and e-mail; I almost never have visitors and don't have to do business lunches. (I take a lunchbox to work and eat at my desk.) After work, I don't entertain businessmen or dignitaries in my home, so having a small house in a quiet neighborhood is fine.

"I don't need a fancy car to drive visitors around. So long as my ten-year-old cars get me the three miles back-and-forth to work, they're fine. Nor do I need an elegant wardrobe: at home and work, I dress casually, eat modestly, and live a simple, lower-middle-class life. My wife and I consider the simplicity of our life a blessing.

"Oh, there are some special *profession-related needs.* Two evenings a week and on Saturdays I freelance as a writer and editor to supplement the income from my day job so I can pay for all those eyeglasses and braces. I've had to set aside one corner of a basement room as an office and furnish it with a simple desk, a computer, and a fax machine. But that was a one-time expense. I don't think I paid more than $700 for all of it. Apart from that, I can't think of any other special expenses my profession demands of me."

Jack's profession requires little more than is already necessary for him to pay for his family's *bare necessities* and *genuine needs.* In terms of his *genuine needs*, Jack with twelve children far exceeds the president with just two; but the president's *profession-related needs* eclipse those of Jack.

Profession-related needs can make a huge difference in how much is enough for each of us, and can force even on private citizens lifestyles that can, from the outside, seem selfish or indulgent.

As an extreme example, Bill Gates built for himself in Washington state a very expensive, high-tech home with music, lighting, and other elements in each room that automatically conform themselves to the tastes and preferences of the persons who enter the room. So technically advanced is this house, and so expensive, that most who hear of it initially dismiss it as a profligate expenditure of vast amounts by a man subject to his whims and so wealthy that he's lost any sense of the value of money and the good that could be done with it were he to devote that same money to the poor.

It may be, however, that Gates built his home this way not merely to delight himself but—as is often the case at World's Fairs and expositions—as a showcase of what the future can hold for all of us, a place to introduce important visitors and potential business partners to what Microsoft has in mind for the future.

I don't know if that is Gates's intention, but if so, then even that very expensive high-tech house could be understood as one of the *profession-related needs* of a man whose job it is to promote the technology that his company sells or hopes soon to sell.

Practicing Detachment

Let's pause for a moment and consider how, the more we examine the idea of genuine need, the more we are brought face to face with our own habits of thinking, good and bad. As we acquire more money in life, it's easy to start thinking that we simply can't do without all the things we have. So to keep our minds sharp and even grow in virtue, it's helpful to learn how to practice a little detachment.

In my own case, for example, I ask—how much money is enough for me?

I've only got one child. I don't spend much more than others for *bare necessities* or even for *genuine needs*. But my *profession-related needs* are heavy: frequent travel, decent clothes, many hotel stays, and a home suitable for entertaining important guests.

In spite of this, I'm not always comfortable with my lifestyle. When I meet some of the people I help through my charities, I come face-to-face with poverty and its dire effects.

I see hungry kids.

I meet grownups who can't read.

I see old folks who are malnourished and mistreated.

I admit that at those times, I grow conscious of my own good health, my excellent education, and the material blessings I have.

I ask myself, "Am I spending my money as I ought? Am I living as I ought?"

Of course, the answer is, "I'm not."

Although I use my wealthy lifestyle as a tool to help others, and I need to live this way to be as effective as I am, I'm sure there are sacrifices I could make so that others would benefit more from what I've received.

I take it one day at a time, and try to keep my conscience engaged.

I remind myself that I'm still a work in progress, and there's a lot more I'm called to do with my life and my money, and that as I come to see more clearly what I should do, I must continue to resolve to do it.

I believe you should take a similar attitude toward yourself.

◆ ◆ ◆

You know, I'm acquainted with a priest who runs a spiritual retreat house in a northeastern state. It's on an estate that was donated to the church by a very wealthy person. Its peacefulness, elegance, and beauty help heal the souls of those who come for a week or a weekend, seeking to restore themselves after being battered by our difficult world.

This priest knows that fine things can be seductive, so even though the retreat house provides him with a grand office and fancy living quarters, every night he sleeps on an uncomfortable cot in a small room he's set up for himself in the garage.

Earlier, I said that I'm still a work in progress. I've come to see the truth in Mary Quant's comment that "Having money is rather like being a blond. It's more fun but not vital."[26]

No, I'm not yet ready to sleep on a cot in the garage, but I do try to remain vigilant. I don't want my *profession-related needs* to become an excuse for a luxurious lifestyle that I choose because I simply want it or, worse, because I think that I deserve it.

In this respect, the president has it easier than I do, and when I start getting comfortable in my wealth, I think of all the perks that come with the presidency and the relation he has to them.

When the president is inaugurated, he inherits the White House

"But can Shirley Temple buy happiness?"

and its elegance, the gardeners, maids and chefs, the limousines, helicopters, Air Force One, and so much more, but—and he knows this from the get-go—they're only his to use, not to have. And he can use them only for a time: four years, or, at most, eight years.

That fact ought to be for him a school of detachment, the virtue that largely inoculates us from the arrogance and possessiveness that can trip up those of us who are surrounded by fine things. For one term or two, the president controls those assets—not, however, as owner of them but only as a trustee: the man who's been offered them so he can fulfill the profession that, for a time, is his alone to fulfill. If he's smart, he keeps in mind the two-thousand-year-old admonition of Marcus Aurelius: "Receive wealth or prosperity without arrogance; and be ready to let it go."[27] He knows that he must use them for that purpose, and then, when his time comes four or eight years hence, instantly and completely relinquish them.

God willing, for more than four or eight more years, I'll have the things that are presently mine and that I presently control; but the years race by and, in the scheme of things, I'm not going to have them all that much longer. Twenty years, forty years: too soon, I'm going to die and, like the president, I'm going to have to instantly and completely relinquish my authority over them, turning them over to those who come after me.

Like the president, I'm just a trustee: a man who's been offered these things so that I can fulfill the profession that, for a time, is mine alone to fulfill. I've got to work to remember that even the things I legally own are, in the deepest sense, really only borrowed for so long as I live. I've got to cultivate the virtue of detachment.

Frankly, whether I'm as wealthy as Bill Gates or as poor as a beggar in India, that seems to me the right attitude to have.

◆ ◆ ◆

What about you and me? What are our *profession-related needs?* How much money do you and I need to pay for them?

Profession-related Needs

To find out how much is enough for our *profession-related needs*, we each have to ask ourselves: "How much does it cost to finance those things I need to fulfill the responsibilities imposed on me by my profession?"

For you and me, how much money is enough?

If we can't afford to pay for our own bare necessities,
genuine needs, and profession-related needs,
and the bare necessities and genuine needs of our dependents,
then we don't have enough money.

And if we're spending our money on *bare necessities*, *genuine needs*, and *profession-related needs*, then we're spending our money as we ought.

◆ ◆ ◆

We began this chapter by asking, "How much is enough for me?" and "Am I spending my money as I ought?" Our path has now brought us the answer to the first question.

We have enough if we can pay for:

✓ *Our own bare necessities*
✓ *Our own genuine needs, and*
✓ *Our own profession-related needs;*

and we can pay for

✓ *The bare necessities of those who depend on us, and*
✓ *The genuine needs of those who depend on us.*

Lack of any of these will keep us and those who depend on us from developing physically, intellectually, psychologically, spiritually, and socially into the morally responsible citizens we're each meant to be, and may keep each of us from playing the productive roles in society we're each called to play.

Do you and I have enough money to pay for our own *bare necessities* and *genuine needs* and the *bare necessities* and *genuine needs* of our dependents, plus enough to pay for our own *profession-related needs?*

Do you and I have a reasonable assurance that we'll be able to afford these *bare necessities, genuine needs,* and *profession-related needs* so long as the obligation to do so remains ours?

If so, then we have enough money.

Beneficial Goods

> *Wealth requires, besides the crust of bread and the roof,—the freedom of the city, the freedom of the earth, traveling, machinery, the benefits of science, music, and fine arts, the best culture, and the best company. He is the rich man who can avail himself of all men's faculties.*[28]
>
> Ralph Waldo Emerson (1803–1882)

Odds are that, like me, you easily passed the test at the end of the last section—you've got enough money.

For most of us, however, the problem with *enough* is that it's only enough: it will get us by, but it's not ideal. In a perfect world, each individual would have not merely enough money but some left over to obtain for himself and his dependents certain "beneficial but not necessary goods" such as those Emerson describes in the following passage:

> To be rich is to have a ticket of admission to the master-works and chief men of each race. It is to have the sea, by voyaging; to visit the mountains, Niagara, the Nile, the desert, Rome, Paris, Constantinople; to see galleries, libraries, arsenals, manufactories.[29]

More than a century after Emerson's death, these remain the privileges of the rich, but they would nonetheless be good for all men and women, as would these other goods that generally improve us as persons and citizens: learning to speak a foreign language and to play a musical instrument, access to fine literature, beautiful art, pleasant and efficient transportation, more than minimal clothing, a varied and interesting diet, a household that's not crowded, and opportunities for pleasant and relaxing recreation.

All of these make an austere life more comfortable and many of them are pleasurable. But they're more than that: they're truly beneficial in that they make it easier for a soul to develop properly. Some of them remove or diminish physical and linguistic barriers between persons; some give the soul solace and necessary rest; some provide that measure of privacy and interior silence that nourishes the deeper elements in men and women; all generally ennoble the person who comes to have them or delight in them. There are the things that, enjoyed rightly, can lead to true and abiding happiness. It's because the rich generally have access to them that Samuel Johnson rightly quipped that "You never find people laboring to convince you that you may live very happily upon a plentiful fortune."[30]

Beneficial they are. They do real good for the soul.

But none of these goods are essential for living a productive, virtuous life. Without them, many a man or woman has become a good person and a wise and productive citizen.

Beneficial goods are those things which are good for us,
but whose lack does not ordinarily prevent us from
becoming the persons—physically, mentally, and spiritually—
that we are meant to be.*

---

* Even so, some of us may choose to embrace a life of austerity regarding material possessions. That seems, however, to be a special calling meant for the few, and not one that should be undertaken by most of us. Mother Teresa's nuns have chosen an austere life, but they also see it as a special calling from God and, knowing how difficult it is physically and spiritually to bear such a life, they practice it only in the tightly controlled circumstances provided them by life in a convent, where the well-being of each can be the concern of all.

◆ ◆ ◆

Generally it's easy to distinguish *genuine needs* from *beneficial goods*. Jack's house is cramped with all those kids. More room would be better for all of them. When I asked him about it, he responded: "Yes, it does get crowded, especially early in the morning on a school day when seven of us are all trying to get quickly into and out of our one small bathroom before we head off to school and work. But we're doing fine. It would be nice to have a larger house and two bathrooms, but we don't really need it. It's probably even good for the kids to have to learn to cooperate. A larger house would be beneficial, but it's not essential that we have it."

◆ ◆ ◆

Earlier we saw that "*genuine needs* are those things that we would be obligated to provide ourselves and our dependents if we had the money." It's clear that dental care for rotted teeth is a *genuine need* and that although a large house for a big family would be better, it's not a *genuine need*. Travel to Europe would enrich Jack and his children, but that's even less necessary than a large house.

Failure to travel to Europe will not seriously impede the

I'm not called to communal life or to such a life of austerity, nor, likely, are you. Nor would it be licit for me to impose it on those who depend on me. Such a life has to be freely chosen or it's likely to warp the person on whom it is imposed.

Chaucer noted in "The Wife of Bath's Tale" in his *Canterbury Tales* that "Poverty often; when a man is low, / Makes him his God and even himself to know." Nonetheless, the fact that wisdom sometimes grows from poverty does not allow us to look away from the genuine sufferings of the poor because we judge that those sufferings just might lead them to wisdom instead of to a life of crime, bitterness, and despair. It's better that those who do not voluntarily choose poverty have sufficient money to provide for their *bare necessities*, genuine needs, profession-related needs, and even *beneficial goods*. Better for them, for their families, and for society.

development of Jack's children. Even if Jack could afford to pay for such a trip for his children, he wouldn't be obligated to do so, nor is he even obligated to let his children go on such a trip if others offer them the means to do so. Thus, our definition expands:

> *Beneficial goods are things that would improve us as persons,*
> *but are not essential to our development. They can legitimately*
> *be denied both to ourselves and to our dependents.*

◆ ◆ ◆

If someone has enough to pay for his own *bare necessities* (food, shelter), his own *genuine needs* (medical care) and his *profession-related needs*, and to pay for the *bare necessities* and *genuine needs* of those who depend on him, then, by the standards we've just enunciated, he clearly has enough money. He's not forced to do without *bare necessities* or, like many people, to choose between one *genuine need* (dental care) and another (eyeglasses).

The problem is that, as I noted earlier, enough is only enough— it's not ideal.

"I admit my cup is full, but it <u>never</u> runneth over."

It doesn't include funds to pay for the *beneficial goods* that will improve us and the way we live, but are not essential to our development.

In struggling to decide whether to send your son to Harvard or to the University of Connecticut, how do you determine whether Harvard is a *genuine need,* a *beneficial good,* or a luxury? If your son is truly called to the Foreign Service, then Harvard would prepare him far better than Connecticut, and going to Harvard would not be a luxury. Under those circumstances, going to Harvard would be at least a *beneficial good* for him, and, might even be a *genuine need*: the education he needs to develop into the person he is called to be.

What if he does go to Harvard and then wants to spend his junior year in Russia?

Again, if he has a strong calling to the Foreign Service, a year of schooling in Russia would certainly not be a luxury but a *beneficial good* because it would help him develop into the adult he seems called to be, able to understand and make prudent decisions about difficult issues in international relations. Indeed, if he really does have such a calling, that year in Russia (or in another major country) might be a *genuine need,* for without it he couldn't develop into the Foreign Service officer he's called to be.

Suppose you determine that Harvard and a year in Russia are for your son not merely *beneficial goods,* but *genuine needs.* In that case, if you have the money, it would not be legitimate to refuse it to your son.

But if you determine that your son's interest in the Foreign Service is less deep and not clearly a calling, then Harvard and a year in Russia remain *beneficial goods* for him. In that case, even if you had the money, you could legitimately finance or refuse to finance one or the other or both.

That may be clearer if you also have another son who's studying accounting. International experience is not nearly as central to his development as an accountant as it is to your other son's development as a Foreign Service officer. A year overseas might be for the accountant a *beneficial good*, but it's not a *genuine need*. Even if you have the money to pay for it, it would be permissible for you to refuse to pay to send him abroad for a year.

Beneficial Goods

To distinguish genuine needs from beneficial goods, ask, "Would it be morally permissible to refuse this, if someone offered to provide it for free, no strings attached?" If it can legitimately be refused—if it is optional rather than obligatory—it's not a genuine need; it's only a beneficial good.

◆ ◆ ◆

Beneficial goods improve the life and character of the person who benefits from them; they leave us better equipped to do the good things we're called to do. Strictly speaking, however, they're not necessary. Without them it's harder, but not impossible, for us to develop fully into the persons we are meant to be and to contribute to society.

If we can't afford to pay for *beneficial goods,* we still may have enough money; nonetheless, it would be better for us to have more—enough to pay for the *beneficial goods* that would make better our own life and character, and those of our dependents.

◆ ◆ ◆

We began this chapter by asking, "How much money is enough?" and "Am I spending my money as I ought?" We saw that the basic concepts of *bare necessities*, *genuine needs*, and *profession-related needs* equipped us to answer the question, "How much is enough?"

Adding to those concepts the notion of *beneficial goods* now equips us to answer the question, "Are we spending our money as we ought?"

The answer now is more nuanced, but not impossible to discern in our own circumstances: unless we have a special calling such as

Mother Teresa's nuns, the money we spend on the following things is being spent as we ought to spend it:

✓ *Our own bare necessities*
✓ *Our own genuine needs, and*
✓ *Our own profession-related needs;*

and

✓ *The bare necessities of those who depend on us, and*
✓ *The genuine needs of those who depend on us;*

and

✓ *Beneficial goods for ourselves and for those who depend on us.*

chapter 4

the *fundamentals* and *non-essential wealth*

It is not he who has many possessions
that you should call blessed:
he more rightly deserves that name
who knows how to use the gods' gifts wisely.[31]
—Horace (65–8 B.C.)

FOR THE SAKE OF BREVITY AND EASE OF REFERENCE, AS WELL AS TO
REMIND US OF THEIR ESSENTIAL CHARACTER, HENCEFORTH LET'S
CALL THE SIX KINDS OF NEEDS AND GOODS LISTED ABOVE THE
FUNDAMENTALS.

> *The fundamentals provide all the things money can buy*
> *to ensure that persons develop as they ought and become*
> *as productive as they can be as individuals and citizens.*

In a perfect world, everyone would have enough money for the
fundamentals.

*"We should consider ourselves fortunate.
At least we have food and shelter."*

In our world (and even in America, the richest country in the world) persons are financially well-off if they have money enough and/or the earning capacity to pay for the *fundamentals* for themselves and their dependents now and hereafter. And insofar as persons—well-off or not—spend their money on the *fundamentals* (giving priority within the *fundamentals* to the ones that come first), then they're spending their money as they ought.

What about money that remains unspent after the *fundamentals* have been paid for and we've made reasonable provision that we'll be able to continue to afford the *fundamentals* for as long as we're expected to provide them?

This is the money that we'll call *non-essential wealth*: money that's not demanded in any way by the obligations inherent in our circumstances and state in life.

Non-essential wealth is the wealth we have left over
after we've provided for the fundamentals insofar
as we're obligated to provide for them.

I have *non-essential wealth.*

You probably do too.

If our *non-essential wealth* were taken from us today, you and I still could fulfill all of our obligations to ourselves and to our dependents, supplying the *fundamentals* for ourselves and for our dependents, for so long as we're obligated to do so.

◆ ◆ ◆

Which brings us back to the question that led us into this discussion in the first place: Can we spare any of our money?

Or, to use the terms we've developed, do we have *non-essential wealth* we can afford to contribute to charity?

What if sending your son to Harvard would be a serious financial sacrifice? If, in fact, your son has a genuine vocation to the Foreign Service, and if, in fact, sending him there would prevent you from providing to your family the *fundamentals,* then, strictly speaking, you have no *non-essential wealth*: it does seem that you really can't spare any.

In that conclusion, however, we come up against one of the limits of our strictly monetary analysis of goods and needs. Beyond the *fundamentals* that money can provide there are many other things we must have if we're to develop into the persons we're meant to become. Among these non-monetary *fundamentals* are love, virtue, and religious faith.

Practicing Detachment (2)

Love, virtue, and religious faith—these topics are more than we're able to consider carefully in this book focused on money, but they're not unrelated to money. As we noted earlier, one form of virtue is *detachment*, the ability to remain clearheaded about all the things we don't need in life, even when they have become so much a part of our lives that we forget what it is like to be without them. Another aspect of detachment is the willingness to sacrifice for another; this is an essential element of virtue and love. In more ways than one, Winston Churchill is right in saying that "We make a living by what we get, but we make a life by what we give."[32] Wise parents nurture in their children the habit of sacrificing for others—a habit that forms children in virtue, develops their character, and provides goods or services to those who benefit from their sacrifices.[33]

Freely giving up things to which we're entitled is one of the non-monetary *fundamentals* that forms us into the persons we ought to become and helps us remain so. Indeed, as we noted earlier, some people deliberately choose to live an austere life largely free of material *beneficial goods* for this very reason. Although as persons they're entitled to certain *beneficial goods*, they refrain from them as a means to gain for themselves virtue, which, in the spiritual realm, is one of the *bare necessities* we must all have: a person who lacks virtue dies spiritually the way a beggar who lacks food and water dies physically.

Even among the destitute—who do not choose their poverty as a spiritual discipline but have it forced upon them—we encounter souls who are ennobled when they give to others money they could legitimately use to pay for their own *bare necessities*. We applaud the spiritual wealth of the woman in the Gospel who had no material wealth:

> And Jesus sat down opposite the treasury, and watched the multitude putting money into the treasury. Many rich people put in large sums. And a poor widow came, and put in two copper coins, which make a penny. And he called his disciples to him, and said to them, "Truly I say to you, this poor widow has put in more than all those contributing to the treasury. For they all contributed out of their abundance; but she out of her poverty has put in everything she had, her whole living."[34]

*"Since I've been dieting, I can sympathize with all these poor
people in India who go to bed hungry every night."*

This Widow's Mite in the Gospel brings us back to our earlier
question.

Judged by dollars alone, someone may have no money to spare
because it all has to go for material *fundamentals*. The problem is
that although materially the *fundamentals* are an easy yardstick by
which to measure the wealth of a man, they're not the measure of
man. In terms of wealth, most everyone who reads this book is
greater than Mother Teresa, but I doubt whether there's one of us
who would claim we are morally or spiritually richer than she was.

So there might be situations where we use some of our money for
something other than material fundamentals, even if, strictly speaking, we don't have enough money even for them. Judged by the
larger standard of one's vocation as a person, it may be spiritually

better for us voluntarily to forgo some of the *beneficial goods* to which, strictly speaking, we're entitled (and perhaps even to forgo some *genuine needs*, particularly if we can bear the burden of those sacrifices) so that spiritually we can become better people.

In this respect, we're no different from the destitute who, as I noted earlier, are also ennobled and perfected spiritually when, from the money that they need for their own survival, they take some small portion and give it to others in need.

Not only is such sacrifice good for souls spiritually; it helps them psychologically. What Lawana Blackwell noted about the very poor applies as well to others who, though not poor, are pressed for cash: they don't feel so poor when they're occasionally able to give.[35]

Later, when we consider the three vocations of those with money, this spiritual dimension of wealth will come to the fore, affording us guidelines we can use to determine how we should relate such spiritual considerations to the strictly monetary *fundamentals* that have held our attention so far.

◆ ◆ ◆

We saw that the president's profession justifies his having a movie theatre in the White House along with sophisticated exercise facilities, a dining room that seats 140 guests, and many other amenities. Although they might initially seem superfluous, these things can justifiably be considered among the *fundamentals* the president rightly enjoys while he is in office.

My *fundamentals* and yours don't include such elaborate facilities, but the demands of your job and mine may well justify a beach house or a mountain cabin where we can relax from the pressures of the week. Insofar as such facilities truly do relax and restore us, such retreats can be justifiable as *beneficial goods* and perhaps, in some cases, even as *genuine needs*. In other words, they may well be for us among the *fundamentals*.

What about building an ultra-modern, high-tech vacation home on 3,000 acres in Portugal with a private, secluded beach? We could add an airstrip equipped to handle jets and then staff it with servants who, every night, would have dinner in the oven and wine chilled and waiting, just in case we fly in from the States without warning.

Maybe you'd like to have a five-hundred-year-old villa in Florence, with red roof tiles contrasting with the brown earth and deep greens of the vineyards that surround it—a villa graced with works by Raphael and Michelangelo.

Some folks could pay for that Portuguese vacation home or Florentine villa without depriving their dependents of any *bare necessities, genuine needs, profession-related needs,* or even *beneficial goods.* But could a Portuguese vacation home or Florentine villa be understood to be among the *fundamentals,* justified because it helps its owner to develop as he ought and become the person he ought to be? Although visits to these overseas homes might, in fact, afford soul-restoring rest and relaxation, homes that cost much less might afford rest in equal measure at a much lower cost.

Now I don't claim here that it's necessarily illicit for Bill Gates— or for you or me—to purchase fine homes (or other non-essential goods that are as costly). There may be reasons that can justify, for some of us at least, such purchases. My point here is only that such things are not among the *fundamentals* on which it's clear we have a right to spend our money. The purchase of such luxuries cannot licitly take precedence over our providing the *fundamentals* for ourselves and those who depend on us. Only if we have sufficient *non-essential wealth* to pay for such expensive luxuries is it permissible for us to purchase them.

◆ ◆ ◆

What if we have that much *non-essential wealth?* That brings us to the question that has troubled me for years, and finally led me to write this book: are there guidelines that you and I must follow in spending it?

Or—since we worked hard to earn it and it's clearly ours—are we completely free to spend our *non-essential wealth* in any way we wish?

Immediately, both you and I say "no."

We're not brazen and crass about our wealth. From our *non-essential wealth* we both give to charities; we hear the cry of the poor and respond to it generously.

But when do we hear it?

Only when we're approached by others?

As the mood strikes us?

And why?

Because it's considered the thing to do in the business and social circles we travel in?

Because we have a vague sense that it's the right thing to do?

Or do we do it from considered principles and according to clear useful standards?

*"It's a real Mohammedan prayer rug.
Of course, we just use it for decoration."*

Indeed, do such standards even exist when it comes to *non-essential wealth*?

◆ ◆ ◆

Obviously, our spending of *non-essential wealth* is not constrained by the *fundamentals* that make claims on the first part of our money—*fundamentals* that, if we're clear-eyed and faithful, guide our hand as we fulfill our obligations to provide for *bare necessities, genuine needs,* and the rest of the needs and goods we've enumerated.

Indeed, in spending our *non-essential wealth* we move into uncharted territory, or at least into territory in which there are no obvious fixed markers to guide our decisions. Like a river in flood time that can go willy-nilly here or there because it's no longer kept in check by its banks, those of us who have ample *non-essential wealth* can afford (financially, at least) to spend it here or there, spend little or lots, and spend it on this thing or that, for good reasons or none.

If we want it, often we can buy it.

And often "I want it" is the only criterion by which we choose whether and what to buy. We go in this direction or that as fashion or impulse move us. We're blown about by the winds of desire and caprice. We're thrust up on strange shores: one year we may find ourselves taken by an enthusiasm for antique cars and the next find it hard to think of anything but the paintings of a famous artist.

So long as we're not doing evil things, is there anything wrong with doing and enjoying the things we like?

I'd like unequivocally to say, "No, it's fine." But the answer is not that simple because *non-essential wealth* can be volatile and dangerous—so much so that it may even literally be better to burn it than to let it remain in our own hands or let it fall into the hands of those we love.

Does that sound overwrought?

Certainly.

For the moment, however, bear with me. Walk with me a few more pages before you turn away. What I'm going to say is not as

"On what floor do I find the hats for better women?"

foreign to you as it may initially sound. With many of the dangers of *non-essential wealth*, you're already acquainted. I'm simply going to look more closely at some of them, and introduce you to a few more tendencies: habits we develop as we spend money, leaving us initially uncomfortable in the doing so, but then, too soon, dulled by habit, accustomed to it.

I'm not talking about the heinous things some folks do with money—supporting the Ku Klux Klan or other nefarious activities that violate rights or corrupt souls. Were you such a person, you wouldn't be reading this book in the first place.

For purposes of this book, I'm assuming that you're an upright person of genuine goodwill, or that, at least, like many who've been blessed with wealth, you genuinely strive to be so. I'm going to focus on those things we do with our money that seem right or at least neutral, but in fact are dangerous—to ourselves, to others, and particularly to those who depend on us the most and who we love the most.

I'll introduce you to these dangers so you'll better be able to recognize them for what they are when next you meet them; and you'll be better able to avoid these dangers to yourself and those you love.

Better yet, I'll show you a way you can largely neutralize precisely those elements of your *non-essential wealth* that pose the greatest danger to the well-being of those you love. I'll show you how to turn your wealth into a school of virtue that will bring you and those you love closer together than ever before.

chapter 5

non-essential wealth
threatens those we love

He does not possess wealth
that allows it to possess him.
—Benjamin Franklin (1706–1790)

ESTATES IN PORTUGAL AND FLORENCE, LUXURIOUS BOATS, A NEW WING ON THE LIBRARY, A 30 PERCENT STAKE IN A NEW BUSINESS: THERE ARE AN INCALCULABLE NUMBER OF WAYS WE CAN SPEND OUR *NON-ESSENTIAL WEALTH*.

Zoos always need substantial help, as do museums, universities, schools, churches, and hospitals. Politicians are always happy to absorb as much of our *non-essential wealth* as the law allows them to take and us to give.

How about flying to Calcutta to knock on the door of one of those hospices run by the religious order founded by Mother Teresa? "Sister," you can say to the Mother Superior. "Here's $100,000. Use it to care for the sick and the dying."

Or we could spend it on ourselves. We're all wounded. We've all suffered. None of us have sufficient *non-essential wealth* to bind the wounds of the world. Why not bind up our own? Push the pain of life out of our days, so at least it can be said that one person spent the last half of his life as free from suffering as one can be?

Then again, maybe we ought just to give our *non-essential wealth* to our kids. They're still young; their whole life remains ahead of them. Why should they have to struggle and suffer as we did? Let them benefit now from our years of hard work. With the head start our money can give them now, they'll suffer less and do far more in the world than we have.

Or should we hold on to our *non-essential wealth* and invest it wisely for as long as we're able? That way, at our deaths our children and favorite charities will receive quadruple what we can give them now.

The good or neutral things we can do with our *non-essential wealth* are endless in their variety, but they really fall into just a few categories, with a couple of variations in each category. We can hold on to our *non-essential wealth* until our death (when we bequeath it to other individuals, to the government, or to charity) or we can get rid of it sooner by spending it, burning it, or giving it away.

Let's consider each of these options, starting with that use of our *non-essential wealth* which is likely to do the least good and cause the most harm. Then we'll review better options, one by one, until we reach that use of our *non-essential wealth* which is likely to bring about the greatest good and cause the least harm.

Along the way, we'll come to understand the meaning not merely of money itself, but of the particular wealth which you and I each have as individuals.

God willing, by the end of our inquiry we'll be able to discern with confidence which uses of our own *non-essential wealth* are not merely good in themselves, but right for us individually, and right for those who are close to us.

We'll be able to answer with confidence the question that can't help but concern us: "Am I using my money as I should?"

Non-essential Wealth Corrupts Many Who Get It

Wealth is the parent of luxury and indolence, and poverty of meanness and viciousness, and both of discontent.[36]

Plato (427–347 B.C.)

Most of us plan at our death or soon before our death to transfer much of our *non-essential wealth* to persons close to us: our spouse, children, and other close relatives. We earned that money; it has served us well, providing a decent life. It seems natural, right, and perhaps even obligatory to pass on to those who are close to us the lifestyle that our wealth has enabled us to enjoy. After all, our obligations to them are significantly greater than our obligations to strangers.

Let's consider whether this is the right thing to do, and if so, how it can be done in a way that brings about for ourselves, for our relatives, and for society the greatest good, while doing the least harm, particularly to those who are close to us.

◆ ◆ ◆

Now one reason not to be quick about giving our *non-essential wealth* to others is that even if it doesn't harm them, they may simply waste it. Three hundred fifty years ago, in his poem "Absalom and Achitophel," John Dryden spoke of a fellow who couldn't keep a grip on his money:

> In squandering wealth was his peculiar art
> Nothing went unrewarded but desert.
> Beggared by fools, whom still he found too late:
> He had his jest, and they had his estate.[37]

Squandering money is a common danger to those who are unused to having and handling significant amounts of it. Like people unaccustomed to foreign travel who call the currency of other countries "funny money," the suddenly wealthy often don't ever develop an inner sense of the money that is instantly theirs. They haven't had, regarding their new wealth, experiences like that of the farmer who has worked for every penny:

The farmer is covetous of his dollar, and with reason. It is no waif to him. He knows how many strokes of labor it represents. His bones ache with the day's work that earned it. He knows how much land it represents—how much rain, frost, and sunshine. He knows that, in the dollar, he gives you so much discretion and patience so much hoeing, and threshing. Try to lift his dollar; you must lift all that weight. In the city, where money follows the skit of a pen, or a lucky rise in exchange, it comes to be looked on as light.[38]

Not having over time come to associate their new wealth with heavy labor or great expenditure of energy to earn it, the suddenly wealthy look on their wealth as light, and find themselves spending real money as if it were play money.

◆ ◆ ◆

If wasting the money was the only problem with giving *non-essential wealth* to others, I wouldn't find it so problematic. Unfortunately, in its benefits and dangers money has great kinship to uranium. When the power in uranium is harnessed and shaped into electricity by persons who are sober, deliberate, conscientious, and skilled, this dangerous substance serves mankind. It lights cities, drives winter cold from the homes of millions, moves heavy subway trains beneath the streets, and powers the phone grid that knits our nation together, one call at a time. Handled properly, "uranium the destroyer" is a great unifier and healer; handled carelessly, its radioactivity sickens and kills those who touch or hold it.

So, too, money.

It bears within itself great power wedded to great danger. "Not the least of its virtues," said George Bernard Shaw, "is that it destroys base people as certainly as it fortifies and dignifies noble people."[39] Handled properly, money improves everything it touches, providing the *fundamentals* to those in need, bringing transportation and health and music and beauty to a world that, without money, would

"Henry, just how much is one hundred billion dollars?"

have no means of gathering sufficient resources to undertake such grand projects.

Misused, however, money seriously damages those who receive it, particularly when those people are young and come into wealth before their characters have been formed in diligence and virtue.

◆ ◆ ◆

The tabloids are full of stories of the failings of other people. Those papers find particularly delectable the turpitude and excesses of the offspring of the rich and famous. I don't know whether the children of the wealthy go bad more often than the children of the poor, or whether cultural fascination with the rich and the famous thrusts errant rich kids into the news more. We do hear about them often—so often that the oddness of it ceases to strike us with the force it should.

Yet it is odd. These kids generally receive the best things money can buy. They grow up in fine homes, get excellent educations, and have the best health care. Their teeth are straight, their skin clear, their hair combed. They never lack the *bare necessities*; they're not deprived of their *genuine needs*; and they receive all the *beneficial goods* the poor yearn to give their own kids. They have all the *fundamentals* money can buy.

What's lacking?

*"My daddy's rich and my ma is good-lookin',
but I'm a mess."*

When a teenager gets caught shoplifting and we read that he's from a broken home in a poor neighborhood, we don't approve, but it does make a kind of sense: by stealing, he's trying to get what he thinks he can't get any other way. Then we read further and find that his companion was a rich kid, just having fun. A poor kid and a rich kid—but not usually kids from decent but modest middle-class households.

*Great wealth and poverty can both be serious obstacles
to the proper moral and spiritual development of the human soul.**

---

* This is not modern phenomenon. Around 350 B.C., Plato described it in *The Republic,* IV, 421B:

   Socrates: There seem to be two causes of the deterioration of the arts.
   Ademantus: What are they?
   Socrates: Wealth, I said, and poverty.

Why is it that?

For the poor, the causes are obvious.

Bad teeth, little education, inadequate medical care, and a poor neighborhood aren't likely to kill the poor; but a life in which obtaining the *bare necessities* is quite difficult and *genuine needs* simply go unfulfilled can cripple or twist souls morally, intellectually, and spiritually. People living in desperate circumstances face severe temptations to anger, bitterness, despair, and the immoral behavior and desperate actions that spring from those feelings or afford temporary respite from them.

Here again we see the truth of James Baldwin's remark: "Anybody who has ever struggled with poverty knows how extremely expensive it is to be poor."

Now in principle at least, money that provides a person's *bare necessities* and *genuine needs* can fend off the evils that can spring from lack of them. Without decent food, good housing, basic medical care, reliable transportation, and a safe living environment, many of

Ademantus: How do they act?

Socrates: The process is as follows: When a potter becomes rich, will he, think you, any longer take the same pains with his art?

Ademantus: Certainly not.

Socrates: He will grow more and more indolent and careless?

Ademantus: Very true.

Socrates: And the result will be that he becomes a worse potter?

Ademantus: Yes; he greatly deteriorates.

Socrates: But, on the other hand, if he has no money, and cannot provide himself with tools or instruments, he will not work equally well himself, nor will he teach his sons or apprentices to work equally well.

Ademantus: Certainly not.

Socrates: Then, under the influence either of poverty or of wealth, workmen and their work are equally liable to degenerate?

Ademantus: This is evident.

Socrates: Here, then, is a discovery of new evils, I said, against which the guardians will have to watch, or they will creep into the city unobserved.

Ademantus: What evils?

Socrates: Wealth, I said, and poverty; the one is the parent of luxury and indolence, and the other of meanness and viciousness, and both of discontent.

us might have fallen into the crimes and vices that shock us when we turn on the evening news.

Clearly, lack of sufficient money to pay for their *bare necessities* and *genuine needs* can deform souls and keep them from developing into the persons they're meant to become.

Unfortunately, the opposite is not true.

Money enough to provide for *bare necessities* and *genuine needs* doesn't guarantee that souls will develop as they should.

Indeed, from time immemorial wealth has had the power to destroy the happiness of the wealthy, a fact mentioned as early as A.D. 100 by Tacitus: "Many who seem to be struggling with adversity are happy; many amid great affluence are utterly miserable."[40] Worse, in some cases wealth actually corrodes souls as quickly and as completely as can destitution.

Non-essential Wealth Stifles Initiative

> *Character cannot be developed in ease and quiet. Only through experience of trial and suffering can the soul be strengthened, ambition inspired, and success achieved.*[41]
>
> Helen Keller (1880–1968)

Destitute people often lack both the skills and the opportunities that awaken hope and prompt initiative. Destitute persons rarely have much control over their situation: they feel themselves at the mercy of the government, the weather, and the whims of those who are richer and more powerful than they. Little seems to make a difference in their lives—for better or worse—so they can grow heedless of consequences. Eat, drink, and be merry for tomorrow we shall die—or, if not "die," then be just as desperate tomorrow as today. Destitution can rob souls of hope and of ambition (which cannot be sustained without hope); destitution too often breeds despair.

Persons who grow up in modest circumstances often—and rightly—come to believe they can alter their own destiny by the decisions they make and the projects they undertake. They know they're not completely immune to the vagaries of weather and to the whims of government and the powerful, but they continue to believe that education and hard work will generally allow them to better themselves. Persons like this who live essentially hand-to-mouth generally feel quickly the consequences of their choices, good and bad. This forms in many of them a habit of attentiveness to decisions and consequences that's often lacking in the destitute whose decisions and actions have little or no transformative impact on their lives.

Placed in circumstances in which they know they can obtain what they seek, but know as well that to do so they have to overcome difficulties not of their own choosing and have to persevere in unpleasant tasks, many lower-middle-class and middle-class young people become self-motivated and learn to persevere. They also come to experience the particular joy known only by those who, after months or years of hard work, attain a goal for which they've long been striving. In middle-class and lower-middle-class young people, the joy of final success after long labor reinforces habits of work and diligence.

When it comes to character formation,
modest circumstances seem generally to be good for young people.

Contrast young people motivated by modest circumstances to rich young people whose *fundamentals* are already provided and who then are given or inherit *non-essential wealth*. Suddenly, they have more money than they need or can spend. Toiling long hours or working many months on a project is not apt to significantly improve their way of life, but it will increase their suffering and stress. Why should they do it?

They may never experience the joy that comes from a hard job well done, or the delight that comes from finally attaining a goal for which they've worked long and suffered much. Because they lack an economic incentive to bear the pain of work, they may never experience the joys of work, and thus wealthy young people, in

*"Everything I have, son, I have because your grandfather left
it to me. I see now that that was a bad thing."*

particular, wind up more susceptible to sloth than people who are
less well off.

Not only can *non-essential wealth* take away the incentive to work
hard, it can insulate young people from both wisdom and delight:
"We learn wisdom from failure much more than from success. We
often discover what will do by finding out what will not do; and
probably he who never made a mistake never made a discovery."*

---

* Samuel Smiles (1812–1904). Emerson made the same point with greater
color: "A youth coming into the city from his native New Hampshire farm,
with its hard fare still fresh in his remembrance, boards at a first-class hotel, and
believes he must somehow have outwitted Dr. Franklin and Malthus, for luxuries are cheap. But he pays for the one convenience of a better dinner, by the
loss of some of the richest social and educational advantages. He has lost what
guards! what incentives! He will perhaps find by and by, that he left the Muses
at the door of the hotel, and found the Furies inside. Money often costs too
much, and power and pleasure are not cheap. The ancient poet said, 'the gods
sell all things at a fair price.'" (Emerson, "Wealth.")

By insulating young people from the bad consequences of their actions, *non-essential wealth* deprives them of one of the very best spurs to solid character formation. It contributes to a habit of indolence: they know that what they do today won't generally make a significant difference in how they live tomorrow. Money will take care of it.

In a word, *non-essential wealth* deprives young people of many of the environmental spurs to ambition they need if they're to become solid, upright citizens capable of contributing to a family and society. And it can keep them from growing in understanding and wisdom from their failures.

This is why we're not so shocked to hear of a poor kid shoplifting or a rich kid joyriding in a stolen car. The poor kid is desperate, doesn't know better, or doesn't care; the rich kid is spoiled, used to taking what he wants when he wants it, and getting away with it.

Non-essential Wealth Impoverishes Humility and Gratitude

Without the rich heart, wealth is an ugly beggar.[42]
Ralph Waldo Emerson (1803–1882)

Poverty has often been romanticized as a gentle state of freedom from attachment to material goods. Unfortunately, that's generally not the case. Destitute people can be among the most desperately acquisitive, and may be attached to the things of this world in ways that are quite unhealthy.

A Russian folk tale tells of a beggar woman who owned just one thing in this world—a potato—which she gripped close to her at all times. The devil came by, saw the potato, and grabbed hold of one end of it.

"Let go of my potato!" screamed the woman, and clutched it tighter.

The devil tightened his grip and headed on down to Hell with it.

"Let go of my potato!" the old woman screamed again, and was dragged all the way into hell.

It wasn't the number or value of her possessions that condemned her; it was that she valued her one material possession more than she valued her life and her soul.

Avarice, envy, and desire plague the poor as much as the rich. Indeed, many a political revolution has been fired more by lust for the goods of the rich than by a genuine yearning for justice. After the overthrow of a wealthy dictator, widespread looting typically strips his homes and offices and the homes and offices of his cohorts. The poor seize what they've long desired but have been denied by the dictator's power.

Even destitute persons not overcome by greed easily fall prey to bitterness, despair, resentment, and anger. Stories from Charles Dickens through the Grimms' fairy tales bring us many examples of bitter and often treacherous poor people, persons whose poverty has left their souls more crippled than their bodies.

Although, as Chaucer noted, "Poverty often; when a man is low, / Makes him his God and even himself to know,"[43] poverty doesn't immunize us against vice or endow us with the virtues of honesty, humility, and gratitude. Often it roots in the poor vices that are harder to dislodge even than the vices of the rich.

While everyone sins, persons of modest means seem not to be as susceptible to money-related vices as are the very poor and the very rich. They have enough to pay for their *bare necessities* and *genuine needs*, but they're not wealthy enough that they can afford all the *fundamentals* or be sure that tomorrow they'll still have enough for them. Today things are fine; tomorrow they may lose their job—and if not tomorrow, then the day after tomorrow. Medical bills may devour what little savings they have, or the old car may break down.

Nonetheless, thoughtful persons in modest circumstances still see that, although they remain vulnerable to fortune, they're doing well compared to many others, at least for the meantime—and this fact alone awakens in the best of them gratitude and other virtues.

Vulnerability is a great spiritual tonic for the attentive soul.

We've already seen how it can keep ambition from flagging. But it can also awaken and sustain a sense of gratitude for the things a person presently has but knows he could easily lose. It helps a person see what is in fact true even of the wealthiest among us: as persons, none of us are truly self-sufficient. Each of us is essentially vulnerable and dependent on others for our well-being. We have to rely on the government to preserve order in society, to maintain public facilities like roads, and to preserve the environment around us. For serious illnesses, we have to depend on hospitals to provide us with medical services. To help us become the persons we're called to be, we need the goodwill of parents, teachers, friends, neighbors, and colleagues.

In thoughtful souls of modest means, recognition that, like all other persons, they're dependent on the beneficence and goodwill of others awakens humility and gratitude, the two virtues that are the fountainhead of wisdom.

Unfortunately, materialism is rapidly transforming the spiritual landscape of our culture and leading the whole population away from the wisdom rooted in gratitude. Too often we see instead greater acquisitiveness, less care for the future, and a growing blindness to the circumstances and needs of others. As psychologist David Elkind notes,

> Many older wealthy families have learned to instill a sense of public service in their offspring. But newly affluent middle-class parents have not acquired this skill. We are using our children as symbols of leisure-class standing without building in safeguards against an overweening sense of entitlement—a sense of entitlement that may incline some young people more toward the good life than toward the hard work that, for most of us, makes the good life possible.[44]

What impact does *non-essential wealth* have on those of us who know that our *fundamentals* are provided? What impact does it have on those of us who know that, without earning another penny, we could nonetheless spend money for years and still not jeopardize our luxurious lifestyles?

Without our realizing that it's happened, having large amounts of *non-essential wealth* can create in any of us the illusion that somehow we're not really vulnerable; we're not dependent on the laws of the nation or even on the laws of the universe to the same extent or in the same way as are those of modest means.

Gertrude Stein compares wealth's insidious ability to narrow our vision to the myopia that enemies induce in us: "The idea of enemies is awful," she says. "It makes one stop remembering eternity and the fear of death. That is what enemies are. Possessions are the same as enemies only less so, they too make one forget eternity and the fear of death."[45]

I have, in fact, met a few individuals whose money and possessions seem to have blinded them in this most ludicrous of ways. Like stupid, spoiled children, they've become almost caricatures. Quite unlike the many generous and hardworking folks who constitute a large proportion of the wealthy today, these few self-important persons have by their bad attitudes and obnoxious behavior fueled for generations the scorn and resentment that too many of the poor and middle class feel for the rich.

The arrogant rich speak proudly of their *non-essential wealth* as a means to thumb their noses not only at those who are less well-off, but at all the usual constraints and conventions that govern men and women in ordinary circumstances. Because money gives them, for a time at least, this freedom, these folks soon succumb to the notion in the old Russian proverb: "It's not money that brings happiness; it's lots of money."

These are the souls who give money a bad name, the ones F. Scott Fitzgerald described in "The Rich Boy":

> Let me tell you about the very rich. They are different from you and me. They possess and enjoy early, and it does something to them, makes them soft where we are hard, and cyni-

JIMMY, SIXTH-GENERATION PAIN IN THE ASS

cal where we are trustful, in a way that, unless you were born rich, it is very difficult to understand. They think, deep in their hearts, that they are better than we are because we had to discover the compensations and refuges of life for ourselves. Even when they enter deep into our world or sink below us, they still think that they are better than we are. They are different.[46] It is about such people that Alexander Pope was speaking when he said, "We may see the small value God has for riches by the people he gives them to."[47]

Now if *non-essential wealth* can awaken arrogance and create a false sense of independence in experienced men and women who should know better, it's even more likely that receiving *non-essential wealth* will trip up young people who have little real experience of this world.

It's not simply true that "dependence upon material possessions

"We must seem like creatures from another world."

inevitably results in the destruction of human character,"[48] but a wealth of material possessions obviously exposes people to many temptations, subtle and not-so-subtle, that are hard to resist.

Rather than growing in humility from the experience of their vulnerability, some young people with ample amounts of *non-essential wealth* come to view themselves as self-sufficient, above the laws of the state and even the laws of morality. That, in turn, can breed in them haughtiness and disdain for others who don't appear to be similarly self-sufficient, particularly the poor and suffering.

When this happens, *non-essential wealth*, particularly in the hands of the young, strangles humility and gratitude, and keeps charity and wisdom from ever blossoming in these souls. It can lead them to lives of profligacy, lawlessness, or even worse. No one would want to give those he loves the means to bring on themselves such consequences.

Non-essential Wealth Threatens Identities

The surest way to ruin a man who doesn't know how to handle money is to give him some.[49]

George Bernard Shaw (1856–1950)

Circumstances are often a major factor in the vocational decisions of persons of insufficient or modest means. One young man goes into the army because it's the best way out of his declining coal mining town; another attends college on a football scholarship because that's the only way he can get a college education; a third quits art school to work at the supermarket because it's the only job she can get and she has to support her divorced and disabled mother.

Not only the very poor, but even persons of modest means often become who they are more because of the opportunities they're given in their limited circumstances than because they're able freely to choose to become just who and what they've always wanted to be.

When such circumstance-molded souls suddenly receive money enough not merely for their *fundamentals*, but *non-essential wealth*, too, they can be unsettled psychologically and spiritually, and sometimes even overthrown.

For the first time in their lives they can choose—unconstrained by external factors—to be who they are and how they will live. Such sudden, simple freedom can lead to an unrecollected and often unhelpful reconsideration of their identity, values, and goals.

Rather than patiently working to discover who they're truly meant to be and then soberly setting out to become that, they often only succeed in abandoning the persons and values they had embraced before they came into money. *Non-essential wealth* can strip them of their stable pre-wealth identity before they have time to establish a stable new identity that's faithful to whom they're meant to be. In that case, new wealth doesn't carry them to the shore they're meant to reach; it shipwrecks them.

The fault lies not in money itself: to think so would be to identify the occasion of the shipwreck as the cause. No, as Seneca saw two thousand years ago, the root of the problem lies deeper: "The acquisition of riches has been to many not an end to their miseries, but a change in them: The fault is not in the riches, but the disposition."[50]

◆ ◆ ◆

Even those who don't suffer an identity crisis find themselves suddenly beleaguered in ways they're not prepared to handle. An old Yiddish proverb says that, "With money in your pocket, you are wise and you are handsome and you sing well too." The fact that others suddenly begin to treat us with greater deference than they did before we had money can lead to an initial period of elation that's then overcome by fear, a sense of isolation, and, finally, cynicism.

In her book *Where Has All the Ivy Gone?* Muriel Beadle comments on how that cynicism corroded the personalities of many of the wealthy with whom she worked: "I developed great compassion for rich people who suspect that they are in demand only because they are a potential source of income to some cause or institution. Whether it's true or not, their suspicions isolate them from all save a handful of old and trusted friends, turn them sour, make it difficult for them to accept new friends at face value, and leave them with little attraction other than their money.[51]

Because money attracts to the wealthy many ungenuine souls and even predators, persons who receive it can grow quickly unsure about where to turn, who to trust, or even how to find out about these things.

◆ ◆ ◆

In many cases the problems go deeper and disrupt not only social relations but even undermine character. For the personalities of some people are fluid, formed not by interior values and will, but shaped by the daily need to provide themselves and their dependents the *bare necessities* and *genuine needs.* Those daily demands force the person to live this way instead of that: to get up in the morning, go to work, persevere through the day, and then return home at night to spouse and children.

When such persons unexpectedly receive great wealth, they're suddenly freed from the financial constraints that to that point had determined the shape of their lives and given them force.

Said Hillaire Belloc many years ago: "I'm tired of Love: I'm still more tired of rhyme. But Money gives me pleasure all the time."[52]

Belloc's playfulness points to a power in wealth that can bring tragedy on those whose lives are flooded with it suddenly: many quit their jobs, try to leave their past entirely behind, and even walk away from their families. For those not accustomed to having and handling *non-essential wealth,* the receipt of money is more often disruptive than not.

Non-essential Wealth Can Lead to Quick Fixes

Money couldn't buy friends, but you got a better class of enemy.[53]
Spike Milligan (1918–2002)

To those who suddenly acquire *non-essential wealth,* it may seem that money can solve almost any problem—without their having to exercise patience, humility, or perform the difficult acts of sacrificial love that actually mend rifts between souls and build strong and loving communities.

Some just walk away from problems with family and friends.

That eliminates the friction, but it doesn't bring about a genuine reconciliation or rebuild the community that has been disrupted. Indeed, by failing to lead all parties to greater virtue and a renewed dedication to work together in friendship and love, wealth may only soften the edges of pain, ensuring that, because the underlying problem remains unresolved, the community will be ruptured further— if not soon in anger then later as unresolved disappointment and distrust cause former friends and neighbors to drift apart.

Young people especially, who suddenly find themselves with *non-essential wealth,* are prone to use money to paper over problems that call for an interior change—problems that are the stuff from which maturity grows in those of us who engage them. Problems that are being papered over or driven away by cash leave the wealthy young person immature, and often even baffled by the failure of their money to win for them the friends and even the love that, initially at least, it seemed to be bringing them. They discover that, as aphorist Josh Billings once put it, "Money will buy you a pretty good dog, but it won't buy the wag of his tail."[54]

Non-essential Wealth Can Bring with It Irrational Guilt

> *A poor American feels guilty at being poor, but less guilty than an American rentier who has inherited wealth but is doing nothing to increase it; what can the latter do but take to drink and psychoanalysis?*[55]
>
> W. H. Auden (1907–1973)

A recent advertisement for an asset management company showed a young girl staring directly at the reader. Her eyes are defiant and vulnerable. Above her, words swirl that set the theme for the whole ad:

*"I'm sorry, but I'm not very good with
children. Here's twenty dollars."*

"Loves having a trust fund/hates feeling guilty about it/loves/hates/
loves/hates/wants a better relationship with money."

We all know of young rich kids whose parents, feeling guilty for
their own negligent parenting, give their children too much money.
When the kids reach twenty-one, they receive the proceeds of a
trust, go from one school to another, study a bit of literature here,
some Zen there, some sort of New Age therapy later. They get ar-
rested for involvement in fashionable anti-war and anti-capitalism
protests. There's a good chance that whatever they're studying or
protesting today, it will be different tomorrow.

Unlike some young people who come into money, these children
were not raised to handle wealth. Because their *fundamentals* are provided, they have no environmental spurs to give them ambition nor
do they feel the need to persevere in any activity that grows difficult,
painful, or even just boring.

Worse, if they come to aspire to an upright life, they slip easily
into moral puzzlement and guilt about their wealth:

"Why," they ask, "have I been singled out to have so much money while some of my high-school friends who work harder than I do, can't even go to college? I have millions to do with as I please, while in the Sudan children die because their parents lack $1 a day to feed them.

"Unmerited, they've been singled out by fate or fortune to die; unmerited, I've been singled out to have millions and no reason to live. If I want, I can buy cars and clothes and jewels and homes and anything else, but I don't want anything.

"What does this mean? Why have they been chosen to die and I to live—and to live lavishly? Should I give them my money? Should I give it to some charity? Or should I just put them out of my mind and live like my parents with their toys? Maybe I should kill myself."

◆ ◆ ◆

I've thought a long time about why some of us have money and others don't, a question that's baffled wise men for generations. But the fact that the question is difficult doesn't relieve you or me of the need to answer it, even if only inadequately.

These questions are more unsettling and dangerous to those who suddenly come into *non-essential wealth* than they are to you and me. Even though we have *non-essential wealth*, the years have filled our lives with daily pressures that give form to our lives. You and I are so tangled up in our daily business affairs that we can even, if necessary, shove such questions out of our minds, or at least postpone them until we get better control of today's business.

Not so those who come suddenly into money. As we saw, *non-essential wealth* can strip them of their former, pre-wealth certainties, leaving them lost and idle. Lacking experience in dealing with money and the understanding of it, they are unprepared to deal with the questions of fate and meaning that money brings with it.

Even persons with experience, character, humility, and self-control who suddenly obtain *non-essential wealth* can be troubled by these questions and bothered by the same doubts, but often they're wise enough to take such questions one day at a time, and deliberately to free themselves of confusion and guilt not by drugs, drink, despair, or suicide, but by working to discover how to transform their *non-essential wealth* from a psychological burden into an instrument that will benefit themselves and others.

It's hard for a young person to respond as well.

Questions about the meaning of sudden or great wealth tend to overwhelm them, bringing confusion, guilt, and even despair. Many of them drown their guilt in pleasure, flee from despair into drugs, drink, or ever more bizarre studies and quixotic causes. Like persons untutored and unpracticed in handling uranium, some souls who suddenly find themselves with large amounts of *non-essential wealth* even die from its effects—generally slowly and painfully.

And, as Emerson notes, even those who don't die are likely soon to find themselves poorer than they began: "It is commonly observed, that sudden wealth, like a prize drawn in a lottery, or a large bequest to a poor family, does not permanently enrich [those who receive it]. They have served no apprenticeship to wealth, and, with the rapid wealth, come rapid claims: which they do not know how to deny, and the treasure is quickly dissipated."[56]

◆ ◆ ◆

Need I say more?

If you and I can provide the *fundamentals* to another person, that's great. But to do more—to give them *non-essential wealth*, now or at our death—may well be the worst thing we could do to another person. All we're adding to their lives is danger.

What justifies that?

Though it may seem selfish, in most circumstances, spending our *non-essential wealth* on ourselves may be better than providing others with *non-essential wealth* that has the risk of seriously harming them.

chapter 6

non-essential wealth
threatens us, too

As I sat at the cafe, I said to myself
They may talk as they please about what they call pelf
They may sneer as they like about eating and drinking,
But help it I cannot, I cannot help thinking
How pleasant it is to have money, heigh ho!
How pleasant it is to have money.[57]
—Arthur Hugh Clough (1819–1861)

THESE DAYS, THERE ARE PEOPLE WHO DON'T HESITATE TO SPEND $25,000 ON A WEDDING CAKE AND A MILLION OR TWO ON A BIRTHDAY PARTY. OTHERS BUY DURABLE GOODS: HALF A MILLION ON A CAR OR A MILLION ON A HANDMADE BEJEWELED SWISS WATCH. SOME BUILD YACHTS THAT COST MORE THAN THE VALUE OF EVERYTHING IN A SMALL TOWN. FOR THOSE WHOSE *NON-ESSENTIAL WEALTH* IS TRULY GREAT, THERE'S ALWAYS THAT ESTATE IN PORTUGAL OR THE VILLA IN FLORENCE, FURNISHED WITH RENAISSANCE ART. AS WOODY ALLEN ONCE PUT IT, "MONEY IS BETTER THAN POVERTY, IF

"Perhaps Monsieur would care for something more expensive?"

ONLY FOR FINANCIAL REASONS,"[58] AND SPENDING MONEY ON ONESELF IS ENJOYABLE.

Fine things bring us pleasure and can bring us prestige. We can even make a kind of ethical argument in favor of buying things for ourselves: if we spend our *non-essential wealth* on ourselves, it won't be there to corrupt our relatives.

And that's surely a kindness to them, though they may not see it that way.

Anyway, it's our money, and we've worked hard for it!

Too many days my business has taken me far from home and family. In a distant place I work a fourteen-hour day, only to wind up near midnight, exhausted in a lonely hotel room. A call to the ones I love just isn't the same as being there, for them or for me.

Long hours, lots of stress, lots of travel: they've earned me lots of money and the right to spend it as I please.

Why doesn't that include spending it on me, if that's what I like?

Will spending money on myself harm me the way it can harm my dependents?

Great wealth can kill their motivation, insulate them from the consequences of their actions, stifle their gratitude and humility, keep them from becoming the persons they ought to become, and generally spoil them.

I'm not convinced that you and I are in the same danger as those who have not worked for their wealth. We may still be working sixty-hour weeks. We may not have given up our stress-filled difficult work weeks, abandoned the many projects that engage us, and launched into a life of leisure. As Edgar Watson Howe said, "If a man has money, it is usually a sign, too, that he knows how to take care of it; don't imagine his money is easy to get simply because he has plenty of it."[59]

Rather than blunting our work ethic, wealth may have sharpened our appetite for productive work—money gives a greater chance to earn a significant return on our efforts, and to do many good things with what we earn. That can spur us to greater efforts to find wise uses for what we've got and to ensure that we don't squander our opportunities through bad decisions or lack of diligence and effort.

But now we're pressing our way through a chapter of this book that promises (in its title at least) to convince us that it could be bad for us to spend our *non-essential wealth* on ourselves. That fact alone shows that you're not someone whose initiative and ethical sense has been blunted by money. You've obviously got enough *non-essential wealth* that it concerns you, and you're genuinely seeking to discover the best way to handle it.

But we both know that we are not immune to the corrupting power of money.

Sure, we may be generally immune to the more public forms of corruption that we see in rich kids gone bad and newly wealthy folks gone wild. But my experience is that we can also get tripped up in ways that are subtler, harder for us to see, and, for that reason, often harder to remedy.

Non-essential Wealth Can Distract Us

Yet the possession of much wealth increases the weight of care, which is a great distraction to a man's mind.[60]

St. Thomas Aquinas (1225–1274)

All of us have hobbies, interests, and activities to which we turn once we've worked enough to satisfy our basic needs. With remarkable perseverance and intensity, whether we're rich or poor, we devote ourselves to non-income-producing activities that interest us: golfing, cooking, writing poems, hiking, stamp collecting, raising dogs, breeding horses, and a myriad of other things we do or have simply because we like them.

In fact, leisure activities are the basis of culture. From them come many of the great accomplishments of mankind—music, literature, art—even though, in your case and mine, we may do them because we enjoy them, rather than in the hope of creating something great.

One of the most marvelous qualities of creation—and of created things—is that things are interesting. If we're not vigilant, our minds get tugged this way and that by them, and without our realizing it, we wind up far from what we intended to be doing. In a charming passage, Emerson speaks of a scholar who steps briefly away from his desk to take a break:

> With brow bent, with firm intent, the pale scholar leaves his desk to draw a freer breath, and get a juster statement of his thought, in the garden-walk. He stoops to pull up a purslain, or a dock, that is choking the young corn, and finds there are two: close behind the last, is a third; he reaches out his hand to a fourth; behind that, are four thousand and one. He is heated and untuned, and, by and by, wakes up from his idiot dream of chickweed and red-root, to remember his morning thought, and to find, that, with his adamantine purposes, he has been duped by a dandelion. A garden is like those pernicious machineries we read of, every month, in the newspapers, which

catch a man's coat-skirt or his hand, and draw in his arm, his leg, and his whole body to irresistible destruction.[61]

Just a walk in the garden caught this scholar by the leg. He was duped by a dandelion! How much more dangerous to single-mindedness are those hobbies and interests which we have ourselves taken up. I know that when I get interested in something, I tend to get drawn into it the way a hapless bug gets drawn down by a whirlpool and swept away.

If I had less money, it would be easier to resist: "I can't afford it" would at least moderate some of my actions.

But I *can* afford it.

Which leaves me—and anyone with *non-essential wealth*—vulnerable to being consumed by interests that are innocent, but may not justify the time and resources we devote to them. There are those who have become so enamored of fine watches that they spend long hours studying time pieces and watchmaking, considering whether to buy the $1 million Swiss watch or the $1.1 million French one with 13 mechanical functions. Others get caught up in wines and can speak at length about the aromatics of a very expensive hundred-

year-old wine of which only three bottles remain in the world. Breeding horses is another hobby of the rich that tends to grow into a whole way of life, with wealth stoking the interest by making it possible for them to buy the finest horses to race or show.

I generally have simpler tastes, but that doesn't keep me from pursuing perfection in more basic things. A few years ago, my wife and I decided to build a summer cottage up at the lake. I can afford to build a cottage in any style I like, large or small, quaint or bold, classic or contemporary. We started by looking at other houses at the lake and then got to reading magazines and books about cottages. We talked to folks, consulted architects, and next thing you know, what we thought would be only a minor project began to consume major amounts of our time and emotion.

The problem is that there are more kinds of cottages and more decisions in the design and construction of them than you and I can reasonably know and master. I'm not complaining, but sometimes while we were having that cottage built, I wished I had less money and had been forced to exclude some options, if only because I couldn't afford them.

Having more than one choice generally improves our lives; but as the number of choices multiply, our lives actually grow more difficult as we struggle to weigh the benefits of one item against the not-quite-parallel benefits of twenty or thirty almost identical ones.

That's the paradox of choice; and it's been aggravated in recent years by the proliferation of variations in even the most basic items.[62] It's not just that the average store has sixty television sets, each with different controls and features, and thirty different exercise bikes, each configured differently. Soon after the fall of the Berlin Wall, a fellow I know took his kids to the toilet paper aisle in his local supermarket and, sweeping his arm from one end of the sixty-foot row to the other, past one brand after another, said to them, "That, my children, is what brought down communism!"

The choices capitalism offers brought down communism, but

they can also immobilize us and consume far too much of our time and energy.

When it comes to things that are too expensive to be found in ordinary stores, those of us who have money are offered many more choices and suppliers than the average person. With more money at stake, and so many possibilities before us, it's easy for us to give to any one decision more time than it deserves.

When it came to building that cottage, my wealth gave me too many choices. Trying to make them thoughtfully caused me more trouble and stress than I needed, robbed me of time, sometimes left me testy, and dragged me away from the things to which I ought to have been paying attention: my family and my business.

Because of what it was doing to me, I actually had to give up day-to-day, hands-on involvement in the details of that cottage.

Did that cottage corrupt me?

Not in the ordinary sense of the word.

In itself, there's nothing immoral about paying close attention to the design and construction of a cottage. There are far worse things I could have been doing with my money, time, and attention. And since I was spending a lot of money on that cottage, it can be argued that I even had an obligation to ensure that my choices were thoughtful, and the construction done right.

The problem is that although there are worse things I could have been doing with my money, time, and attention, there are also better things—such as devoting myself to my family, my business, my church, and my community.

About the cottage, I lost the virtue of detachment I should have had. It assumed more importance in my mind than it had in reality. I got so wrapped up in the project, that, for a while at least, I took my eye off the ball when I was dealing with more important things.

I lost my edge.

And that's never good for folks like you and me.

Before I did serious harm, I pulled back and wrenched myself away from that cottage to resume the more important things for which I was responsible. But it stands as a reminder to me that *non-essential wealth* can sometimes be as much of a hindrance in life as a help.

I've met many others who have had similar experiences. Some got involved with wines, devoting long hours to the study of viniculture and hundreds of thousands of dollars building the perfect wine cellar; others became opera connoisseurs and traveled the world to hear the best tenors in the best houses; some spent millions and all their spare time on antique cars or fine thoroughbreds.

In themselves, these are innocent amusements. But all of them tended to draw these folks away from the things that ought to be at the center of their lives: their families, their work, and their community.

◆ ◆ ◆

Are middle-class folks and the poor immune to such fascinations and consuming involvements?

Not at all.

I know of one middle-class household filled with Mickey Mouse items—Mickey Mouse telephones, Mickey Mouse napkins, Mickey Mouse bedspreads, and black-velvet Mickey Mouse paintings on the walls.

Other people furnish their homes completely with NFL items.

Can this be all-consuming? Yes.

But ultimately not as dangerous as such obsessions can become among those of us with more money.

Even though we may think these people ought to use their money differently, at least their circumstances force them to disengage themselves from the things they own and want to do. They must go to work every morning, and pay full attention to their jobs, otherwise they'll lose those jobs and their cars and their homes.

Now I don't mean to suggest that poorer folks are more likely than wealthier ones to have the virtue of detachment, and to value things as they ought to be valued, always remembering that, in the grand scheme of things, their possessions are only lent to them for a while and will be taken from them at death, if not before. We saw already that though she owned only a potato, that poor old woman was dragged into Hell by it, because about that potato she had no detachment whatsoever.

It's not that the poor are more detached than the wealthy; it's that their circumstances place natural limits on the impact that their goods and interests can have on their lives.

In this respect, for us as for them, the limiter is essentially the same: "How much can I afford?"

But since our *non-essential wealth* enables us to afford so much, those of us who have it are indeed vulnerable to being drawn more

"Of course, money does have its advantages. When we first bought this place, that hill was on the right, but Morton didn't like it there, so he had it moved over to the left."

deeply into such activities than is good for us or reasonable. Sometimes we get so involved that we grow lax about our daily business and family obligations, and may even come to see both as obstacles to our pursuing the more interesting activities that our *non-essential wealth* allows us to pursue.

When this happens, our *non-essential wealth* has become as corrosive of our souls as we've seen it can be to the souls of the immature and the newly wealthy. We have become the person that Ben Franklin had in mind in the passage we quoted earlier: "He does not possess wealth that allows it to possess him." If we are at all vulnerable to such temptations, then it would be better for us to rid ourselves of our *non-essential wealth* than risk succumbing to these seductive forces that are inherent in it—forces that can divert our attention and affections from the things that ought to be most important to us: faith, family, community, and work.

Non-essential Wealth Can Increase Frustration

> *You don't seem to realize that a poor person who is unhappy is in a better position than a rich person who is unhappy. Because the poor person has hope. He thinks money would help.*[63]
>
> Jean Kerr (b. 1923)

There's another but less innocent way that *non-essential wealth* can trip us up.

I travel a lot, both for my business and with my family. In big cities the accommodations are fine, but in small towns I can wind up in a motel by the side of the freeway.

The taxi drops me at the front door. I carry my suitcase into the lobby and stand at the desk for two minutes while the clerk ignores me. After getting my key, I go on down to my room, which is dark and chilly. I walk over to the heater, turn the knob to get it running, and the noisy blower shoves dust into the air and then heat.

It's one of those loud heaters that turn on and off frequently, struggling all night to maintain an even temperature. At least when it's on, it will block out some of the noise from the trucks rushing past. I walk over to the window, open the curtains to let some daylight into the room and find myself face to face with . . . a dumpster, just six feet outside my large plate glass window.

All right.

I won't complain.

That's what I've got to expect when I stay in a motel by the side of the road, even if it's the best motel for fifty miles around.

Conditions are different in New York, San Francisco, and the bigger cities, and my expectations are different, too. After a long flight and a tense ride through rush-hour traffic, I arrive at the city's finest hotel where the doorman opens the door for me and gets my luggage from the trunk. At the desk in the richly appointed lobby, a soft-spoken but very efficient clerk checks me in. As the smooth, swift, silent elevator whisks the bellman and me up to my twelfth-floor suite, I feel my expectations rising and the taut muscles in my shoulders starting to relax: it's going to be a comfortable, quiet evening before that challenging meeting in the morning. That's what I need right now.

The bellman unlocks the room for us and I notice that the lights are already softly lit, and the room warm. The heater is whisper silent and the temperature will be even all night long.

Now this is more like it!

After the gracious bellman retires with his tip, I walk past the polished mahogany desk to the window and open the curtain to let some light into the room and find myself face to face with . . . the fire escape of a tenement just sixty feet away!

What?

I'm paying $800 a night to look at a tenement fire escape!

I won't take that, and you wouldn't either.

Almost immediately, my mood veers from contentment to anger.

I'm on the phone to the front desk only to hear from the clerk that the hotel is full and there are no other rooms available.

Now I'm really irritated.

Truth is, because I expected less from that roadside motel with the noisy heater, I was less troubled there and more gracious to the workers, even though the accommodations were almost substandard and the clerk was less gracious to me.

I've found that in some ways, fine hotels—and other fine things—are snares that sometimes catch me unawares. They awaken in me greater expectations, which leave me more easily disappointed and more quickly upset when they aren't what I thought I was paying for.

One time at breakfast, room service charged me $50 for breakfast but forgot to bring the bacon I'd ordered with it.

Fifty bucks for breakfast and they forgot my bacon!

I could have done better at the breakfast buffet at the roadside motel.

And that was free.

That $50 breakfast got me agitated, and colored the rest of my morning.

Was I just being bratty, or was my indignation justified?

For that kind of money I had a right to expect perfection.

Which is just my point: more than the poor and the middle class, you and I suffer the negative consequences of:

The Law of Rising Expectations
The more we expect from something,
the more vulnerable we are to disappointment
and the unhappiness and vices that come from it.

In our case, the more money we have, the more money we tend to pay for goods and services. And the more we pay for them, the more we tend to expect from them. In the $89-a-night motel we're not troubled by the dumpster view and half expect room service to forget the bacon; but we find those infelicities intolerable in the $800-a-night room. In a room fit for a king, we wind up frustrated, agitated, and angry.

"Front desk? There are no little candies on my pillow."

About what?

Bacon.

Which is not, in the scheme of things, all that important; and we even know it at the time.

◆ ◆ ◆

About buying happiness, Larry McMurtry once said that "No illusion is more crucial than the illusion that great success and huge money buy you immunity from the common ills of mankind, such as cars that won't start."[64]

Unfortunately, more money doesn't free us from the consequences of the Law of Rising Expectations; it aggravates the problem by increasing our desires, leaving us more vulnerable to the Law and its consequences. The ancient sage Seneca says it well:

> Imagine that you've piled up all that a veritable host of rich men ever possessed, that fortune has carried you far beyond the bounds of wealth so far as any private individual is concerned,

building you a roof of gold and clothing you in royal purple, conducting you to such a height of opulence and luxury that you hide the earth with marble floors—putting you in a position not merely to own, but to walk all over treasures—throw in sculptures, paintings, all that has been produced at tremendous pains by all the arts to satisfy extravagance: all these things will only induce in you a craving for even bigger things.[65]

Not only that, but as our wealth grows, it outstrips the abilities of humans consistently to provide goods and services proportionate to our increased wealth. In any ordinary lodging, $5 will buy me hot bacon and cold orange juice; in a fine hotel, $50 should get me the same. Suppose I wind up in a place that charges $500 for orange juice and bacon. That's a hundred times what orange juice and bacon cost in a cheap hotel, and ten times what they cost me in a fine one. But they're not going to be prepared and delivered by people who are respectively a hundred times more competent than in the cheap hotel and ten times more competent than in the fine hotel.

In these things, you just can't increase human competence to the same degree. No matter where we go, we'll be dealing with human beings; and no amount of training and breeding can magnify competence at the rate and to the scale that you and I can magnify what we pay for things.

Which means that sometime, somewhere, I'm going to pay $500 for bacon and orange juice and I won't get my bacon.

I'll be furious.

$500 and no bacon?

◆ ◆ ◆

But you know what?

It's still just orange juice and bacon.

In situations like this, I have to keep reminding myself of that.

And I have to work to remember that mistakes are what we've got to expect of our fellow men, even in fine hotels. They're going to screw up sometimes the way you and I screw up sometimes. There's no amount of money that can insulate us from the foibles and mistakes of other human beings.

Another law—the Law of Diminishing Returns—guarantees that as we pay ever more money for services, we always reach a point where our increased expenditures simply increase the disproportion between how much we pay and what we get.

That, in turn, heightens the odds that we'll be disappointed and the likelihood that we'll lose our patience or even our temper, and castigate someone more harshly than they deserve.

I know, because I've done it.

I've been less gracious with workers in fine hotels than with less competent workers in roadside motels.

They're always well-trained and act concerned, but that may only be so they can keep their jobs. Likely they see anyone who can pay $50 for orange juice and bacon as spoiled. I'll deal with that later.

But even the least paid among them can understand what frustrates me and would frustrate them, too: the disproportion between what I paid for and what I received.

Unfortunately, the Law of Diminishing Returns doesn't merely apply to services; it applies to goods, as well. Once we reach a certain level of quality, which usually is not very expensive to reach, spending more money buys more bells and whistles but generally doesn't get us that much more quality. We pay a few thousand dollars for a television that gives us an excellent picture at the screen-size we like. Paying 50% more may give us a sophisticated remote control and special screen-splitting capabilities, but doesn't generally improve the image quality one bit. We pay less than a thousand dollars for a durable clothes washer that gets our clothes as clean as they can be gotten. For 50% more, we can buy a model that has electronic switches instead of mechanical ones, and offers more washing options (which we probably won't ever use)—but the more expensive machine doesn't get our clothes one bit cleaner.

In both cases, the 50% increase in price doesn't bring us a 50% increase in value: like the services we pay for, goods also generally are bound by the Law of Diminishing Returns.

The Law of Diminishing Returns applies as well to cars and homes and boats and the other big-ticket items that, before we have them, promise to make us significantly happier. A ten-thousand-acre estate offers ten times the rivers and fields of a thousand-acre estate, and could well cost us more than ten times what the smaller one would. But there's no way—apart from devoting ourselves to it as a full-time job—that we can enjoy all nine thousand additional acres: it's humanly impossible.

In terms of enjoyment, and before we ever move in, the Law of Diminishing Returns ensures that the proportionately greater cost of the larger estate will not bring us proportionately greater delight.

Worse, when the larger estate first caught our eye, our expectations of enjoyment there rose sharply. For months as we negotiated its purchase we forgot to stay mindful of the Law of Rising Expectations, which guarantees that the greater our anticipation becomes, the more vulnerable we are to disappointment, even with grand things like a ten-thousand-acre estate.

Or should I say, "especially with grand things like a ten-thousand-acre estate"?

Only those who have the time and capacity to devote themselves exclusively and single-mindedly to such things—which is not me and not likely you—are ever going to be able to hold at bay the negative consequences of two Laws that conspire to rob our *non-essential wealth* of much of the delight that we hope to wring from it: the Law of Diminishing Returns and the Law of Rising Expectations.

No wonder John Ruskin concluded that "Every increased possession loads us with new weariness."[66]

Now I grant that diminishing returns and increasing frustrations are not compelling enough to lead most people to refrain from spending their *non-essential wealth* on themselves. Most of us are willing to put up with these negative consequences in order to enjoy

"Cosgrove, I just bought that damn building, right? So you'd think I'd be happy, right? Well, I'm not happy. How do you figure that out?"

the pleasures of the things we can afford—bacon and orange juice— even when we know that the finer those things are, the more they subject us to a level of frustration greater than that experienced by many of lesser wealth. This is so even when we remember (as happened with my cottage at the lake) that spending our *non-essential wealth* on ourselves can cause us to lose our focus, take our eye off the ball, and tangle us up in things to which we really ought not to devote so much time and energy.

I mention these not as conclusive arguments that it's a bad idea to spend your *non-essential wealth* on yourself. I merely ask you to stop the next time you find yourself disappointed by that thing for which you paid so much, or when you find yourself losing your patience because even your wealth wasn't able to get you bacon and orange juice when you wanted it. Instead of getting caught up in the frustration of the moment, ask yourself whether being shed of *non-essential wealth* spent on yourself might actually make your life easier.

A hundred years ago, John D. Rockefeller considered just these points, and came up with a novel solution:

> The mere expenditure of money for things, so I am told by those who profess to know, soon palls on one. The novelty of being able to purchase anything one wants soon passes, because what people most seek cannot be bought with money. These rich men we read about in the newspapers cannot get personal returns beyond a well-defined limit for their expenditure. They cannot gratify the pleasures of the palate beyond very moderate bounds because they cannot purchase a good digestion. . . . As I study wealthy men, I can see but one way in which they can secure a real equivalent for money spent, and that is to cultivate a taste for giving where the money may produce an effect which will be a lasting gratification. . . .[67]

Non-essential Wealth Can Amplify Other Personality Flaws

> *Money doesn't change men, it merely unmasks them. If a man is naturally selfish or arrogant or greedy, the money brings that out, that's all.*
>
> Henry Ford (1863–1947)

At work, the businesses I engage in are generally so intense that I just don't have time to struggle with a recalcitrant laser printer or wait for a program to load in a slow computer. And because so much of my work spills into the evenings—and I do need to have time with my family—I don't have time at home to fix light switches, mow the lawn, or devote lots of time and attention to furnishings or elaborate entertainments.

For the sake of my family (and efficiency, too), I've chosen to live well but not extravagantly, both at home and at the office. I hire good people; I buy good tools; at home and at work I expect these things to serve me well.

Although my home and office are deliberately less lavish and more functional than a fine hotel, I've paid a decent amount of money to ensure that they afford me the same kind of hassle-free experience I expect to get in a fine hotel: hassle-free, but not elegant.

Pleasant efficiency is the standard by which I've judged how to build, furnish, and staff both work and home. It serves me well, not only in getting things done but in helping me keep a check on my emotions when I find myself growing frustrated: I remind myself that losing control will interfere with the very goals I hoped to achieve by creating spaces and hiring a staff geared toward pleasant efficiency.

In effect, since my office is geared toward an end beyond itself—the accomplishment of our goals as a business—there I have some protection against the soul-corroding effects of the Law of Rising Expectations.

Suppose, however, I'd not arrayed my offices for the good of the business, but rather had spent lots of money there on things to please me. At those times when I found myself displeased, what external check would there be to my impatience and anger?

Not pleasant efficiency, for that's not what I sought to purchase with my money. It seems to me that if I sought to purchase items which pleased me—that is, if my pleasure was the standard by which I judged things—then the only thing that could quiet my impatience or anger would be getting that which pleased me.

An office—or any other place or organization—measured by what pleases or displeases me leaves me without any external checks on my attitudes and actions; it leaves those who deal with me without any external standard by which to judge what to do or not do next. Even pleasant efficiency is not there to moderate my moods and subdue impatience. I'm left at the mercy of my whims and moods, as are those who have to deal with me.

When we fall into the habit of spending our money simply on

"I don't have to be a team player, Crawford. I'm the team owner."

goods and services that please us, regardless of their value or importance in and of themselves, we wind up isolated in ourselves. We're more likely to be dominated by unpleasant personality traits that would be moderated if we sought to govern our moods and actions by an objective standard.

It is this phenomenon that gives credibility to the claim that money amplifies personality flaws. That amplification is not a necessary complication of money, but it's a common one in those who have sufficient money to spend it according to their whims and desires, and not in order to achieve ends outside themselves.

Non-essential Wealth Invites Vanity Spending

> *Quarterly, is it, money reproaches me: "Why do you let me lie here wastefully? I am all you never had of goods and sex. You could get them still by writing a few checks."*[68]
>
> Philip Larkin (1922–1986)

As I said, in relation to the money I have, I live what I believe is a fairly modest lifestyle. Yet because I have a more comfortable

"Here is a car that is not the least bit afraid to say, 'I cost plenty.'"

life than most people, some might call my way of life lavish and wasteful.

To keep my mind clear about why I make the choices I do and live as I do, I frequently review my recent activities and purchases and ask myself the following question (and I suggest you do the same, regularly):

> *Although I know that my wealth is not the measure*
> *of my worth, am I sustaining a level of consumption that can*
> *only be explained as an effort to impress others with my money*
> *and social status?*

Sometimes I discover that certain of my purchases and activities did not really further my core values but were made to impress others. At those times, I take a breath and resolve to focus better on what I should have done, and to do better tomorrow. I resolve for the hundredth time to remember that my wealth is an opportunity rather than a means to indulge myself.

It's common knowledge, but that doesn't mean we can leave it unremarked here: having a better car or fancier boat doesn't make anyone a better person. Pleasure and comfort are not the measure of a man—not even greater pleasure and comfort than others have.

We both know that, so I won't dwell on it, other than to say that although young people are more likely to fall into this error, you and I do it, too; and we need to be vigilant against it. It's a perennial danger of having *non-essential wealth.*

Non-essential Wealth Imposes No Intrinsic Limit on Spending

Riches enlarge, rather than satisfy, appetites.
Thomas Fuller (1608–1661)

I briefly tasted the limitlessness of desire when, in my mind, I was building my cottage at the lake. The more I thought about it, the more possibilities opened before me and the more appealing they became. I found myself on that treadmill Maimonides spoke of almost a thousand years ago,

> You desire to have your vessels of silver, but golden vessels are still better; others have even vessels of sapphire, or perhaps they can be made of emerald or rubies. . . . Desire is without limit, whilst things which are necessary are few in number and restricted within certain limits.[69]

Now the problem of ample *non-essential wealth* is that it doesn't merely invite us to entertain limitless desires, it tempts us to seek their fulfillment. Why shouldn't I have vessels of silver, or gold, sapphire, emerald, or rubies? Why not vessels of all five materials? What's to limit me to one or even two of them?

Only what I want.

Only desire.

I have fought against desire many a time, but it never dies completely. Emerson finds the battle futile: "It is of no use to argue the wants down: the philosophers have laid the greatness of man in making his wants few; but will a man content himself with a hut and a handful of dried peas? He is born to be rich."[70]

But if desire is limitless and no other controls are imposed on those of us with *non-essential wealth*, will we not be consumed by the effort to fulfill those limitless desires? Almost every nation has somewhere in its history the story of men or women who have become legends for trying—and failing—to fulfill their every desire. Almost every nation has somewhere in its lands a castle or palace that stands as a monument to the ostentatious kind of human folly that seems to overtake those who have so much *non-essential wealth* that it allows them to attempt to match material goods to the desire they have: the 250-room Biltmore estate in North Carolina (the house alone covers four acres), the 165-room Hearst mansion in California, Versailles in Paris, Neuschwanstein in Germany, the Taj Mahal in India, even the pyramids in Egypt.

If those who created these grandiosities were not surfeited with *non-essential wealth*, they never would have attempted these undertakings. Having great *non-essential wealth*, they found in it no intrinsic limits to what they could or should attempt.

Would it have been okay for the Vanderbilts to have constructed

"We had these twigs flown from Italy"

Biltmore with only 125 rooms or for Hearst to have cut back to just 100 rooms for his house?

How do you determine what is excess and what is not? The problem is that, as Emerson noted, "Want is a growing giant whom the coat of Have was never large enough to cover."[71] If you let desire be your guide, you'll never find a limit; and the problem is that *non-essential wealth* tempts you to do just that. Too easily the question slips from "why should I do it up so grandly" to "why not?"

> *Only the amount of money we need for the fundamentals*
> *affords a reliable limit on spending, freeing it*
> *from the whims of desire.*

We saw earlier that wealth devoted to the *fundamentals* can be justified. Good reasons can be given for those expenditures and, within limit, we can discern the kind that are licit and their limits.

That's not the case with expenditure of *non-essential wealth* on oneself.

Non-essential wealth is non-essential precisely because it's more than will be needed for the *fundamentals*; it surpasses the bounds of what is called for by the *bare necessities* of life, by *genuine needs* and even *profession-related needs* and *beneficial goods*. It is vulnerable to desire and desire is vulnerable to it—precisely because desire is the only thing that can claim it.

There is nothing intrinsic to *non-essential wealth* that calls for a limit on spending. Therefore, in principle at least, if desire is the criterion, there is no limit: if I want it, I buy it, and my desire to buy it is reason enough for me to buy it.

That is the triumph of selfishness.

Is that who we want to be?

Non-essential Wealth Promotes Pseudo-resolutions of Real Problems

Sir, money, money, the most charming of all things; money, which will say more in one moment than the most elegant lover can in years. Perhaps you will say a man is not young; I answer he is rich. He is not genteel, handsome, witty, brave, good-humored, but he is rich, rich, rich, rich, rich—that one word contradicts everything you can say against him.[72]

Henry Fielding (1707–1754)

Our discussion of the *fundamentals* identified real needs and goods to which we should devote our wealth. In each case, those needs and goods were things that promote the proper development of the human persons who are their beneficiaries: food, shelter, education, medical and dental care, even formation to fulfill a particular vocation in life. Without the *fundamentals*, human beings don't do well; with them, human beings have a chance to flourish.

Money generally goes a long way toward providing *bare necessities*. Even many *genuine needs* can be bought: shelter, warmth, medical and dental care. Other *genuine needs*, however, are rooted in values, not things. Providing them requires more than money. Among these are emotional and intellectual relations with others—particularly adults—and moral and spiritual development. These values don't sustain bodies, they form character.

Character enables us to evaluate situations, to choose the right and prudent course of action that will bring about good fruits today and in the future, and, by valuing that which should be valued and shunning that which should be shunned, to build an enduring community rooted in compassion and justice. Character can't be bought; it has to be learned, generally from bearing suffering and hardship.

Parents who use their money to keep their children from the hard work and sacrifices that build character do their children no good, leaving them vulnerable later to problems that can't be fixed with money. Parents who buy their children the latest styles and get them the most popular games and toys to help them win friends do their children no good.

Grownups who overcome disagreements or depression by buying things—for themselves or others—may assuage their pain for the moment, but a new car or a new house won't give meaning to a universe that seems to be meaningless, or reconcile a man and wife who use their money to keep from confronting and resolving fundamental issues that have arisen between them.

Then there's the problem of friendship and love: free-spending can create the illusion of both by keeping people near to us who, when we run out of cash, will quickly go elsewhere.

Wisdom comes from genuine encounters with the world and others in it, encounters that too often are painful. Nonetheless, bearing pain for the sake of wisdom and the community it builds is preferable by far to throwing money at problems, which, especially in

"Now all we need is something for when he's opened all his presents."

times of frustration, offers itself as a pseudo-solution to those of us who can afford to do it.

Papering over problems with money is just another way of spending money on ourselves. It diminishes us when we attempt it. It leaves us more isolated and unhappier than before. It risks making us into one of those wretched monied souls about whom Samuel Johnson said three hundred years ago, "All this [wealth] excludes but one evil—poverty."[73]

In a word, spending our *non-essential wealth* on ourselves is hazardous. It's time to consider ways we can use it that aren't hazardous—that are, in fact, good.

chapter 7

money is good

Do not say to yourself, "My power and the might of my own hand have gotten me this wealth." But remember the LORD *your God, for it is he who gives you power to get wealth, so that he may confirm his covenant that he swore to your ancestors, as he is doing today.*
—Deuteronomy 8:17–18

A S I WAS WORKING OUT SOME OF THE IDEAS PRESENTED HERE, I SUGGESTED TO A FRIEND THAT IF WE'RE TO BE EXHAUSTIVE IN OUR CONSIDERATION OF THE THINGS WE CAN DO WITH *NON-ESSENTIAL WEALTH*, WE HAVE TO INCLUDE LITERALLY SETTING FIRE TO IT. "ALTHOUGH THAT'S THE LEAST ATTRACTIVE ALTERNATIVE . . . ," I STARTED TO SAY BEFORE MY FRIEND CUT ME OFF: "FRANK, YOU JUST ARGUED THAT *NON-ESSENTIAL WEALTH* THREATENS YOUR DEPENDENTS AND EVEN THREATENS YOU. HOW CAN BURNING IT BE WORSE THAN THAT? ISN'T BURNING IT BETTER THAN RUINING YOUR OWN LIFE WITH IT AND BETTER THAN RUINING THE LIVES OF THOSE YOU LOVE?"

His point jarred me.

It's counterintuitive.

"With money, we can make the devil push a millstone."[74]

With money, we can retain a host of workers to serve in our houses and maintain the grounds for us. We can feed the poor, build hospitals, make movies, and travel. We can construct factories and establish companies that create new drugs that save many lives.

Money gives us power over resources—material and human. It gives us the power to direct the development, management, consumption, and disposition of resources.

And lack of wealth can leave us helpless in the face of man and nature.

Annually, floods drown the destitute in Bangladesh who are too poor to move out of the floodplain of the Ganges River or to build houses strong enough to endure the floods. Lack of money leaves them helpless against the floods.

Old people too poor to move out of crime-ridden neighborhoods suffer indignities and sometimes death at the hands of brutes and thugs. Lack of money denies them the power to live in safer neighborhoods.

In the face of the capricious forces of nature and man, it's better to have power than not. Where evil would triumph, wealth may bring about the triumph of good. Those who casually criticize the having of wealth forget the power for good that lies in wealth.

No wonder we instinctively shrink back from the suggestion that we set fire to our money, no matter how much or how little we have. Burning money squanders the power it gives us to shape our lives and those of others. Burning money shrinks opportunities, limits choices, and leaves us more vulnerable to the whims of time and chance and circumstance.

Destroying wealth is wasteful.

Literally, it's a reversal of fortune.

"But," my friend came back at me again, "which is worse? To squander money by burning it or to squander our own lives—our own lives and the lives of those we love—by letting our *non-essential wealth* ruin us?"

*"And I happen to know they won't let you take them
with you down there, either."*

*Wealth, like fire, is one of the greatest goods ever given to mankind;
indeed, rightly used, it has power to bring about goods
much greater than fire ever brought.*

It's true that if that fire threatens the person who plays with it,
he'd better not play with matches; and if wealth threatens the soul of
the person who has it, he needs to get shed of that wealth. Later,
we'll speak of prudent ways that can be done.

But, because of the great good that fire and money can bring
about, we ought not to lightly or immediately turn away from the
gift of fire—or from the gift of money that has been given to you
and me. We ought not without a struggle quickly destroy this great
instrument for good that has been put into our hands. First, we

should determine if there is a reason why it has been put into our hands in particular, and not into the hands of another person.

We need to find out what it means that you and I have money, and others do not.

Can it be that God or Providence or Chance merely intends to bestow on me the means to have greater ease and pleasure?

Have I been singled out by the universe to take it easy?

If so, why?

What have I done to deserve to be pampered while others, not far from here, fall asleep hungry, or die destitute in the streets of Bangladesh?

Can that be the meaning of my money: that I have a good time while others suffer?

If self-indulgence is the meaning of our wealth, then self-indulgence is all we lose when we destroy our wealth to keep it from harming us morally. That's not a bad trade: we often sacrifice pleasure and self-indulgence in order to achieve a greater good for ourselves.

*"Researchers say I'm not happier for being richer,
but do you know how much researchers make?"*

But suppose there is a larger purpose for the money we destroy? Suppose it's meant for far more than our own comfort?

Would it be right to destroy an instrument put in our hands to do good?

The smart solution isn't to eliminate fire—or wealth— but to use them safely, and as they ought to be used. Wealth is good.

Money Facilitates the Transfer of Goods and Services

Money is not, properly speaking, one of the subjects of commerce; but only the instrument which men have agreed upon to facilitate the exchange of one commodity for another. It is none of the wheels of trade: it is the oil which renders the motion of the wheels more smooth and easy.[75]

David Hume (1711–1776)

Wealth comes in many forms, of which money is only one, but a very important one because it affords a clue to the meaning of other forms of wealth.

Primarily, money is a medium of exchange that eases the transfer of goods and services between persons. Instead of trading my cow for your wagon so I can drive the wagon down the road and trade it for a plow and then hoist the plow on my back and walk down the path to the grocer (who's looking for a plow) and trade the plow to him for food, I simplify the process by selling my cow for money and using the money to pay the grocer. With fewer transactions, I achieve the same result: I transform the value of my cow into groceries. In this way, money eliminates friction in the system. By facilitating the exchange of goods and services, it enables us, with the same effort and expense, to engage in more exchanges than we would otherwise be able to engage in profitably. And by doing so, money increases the number of transactions that occur. In itself, money promotes commerce.

But it does more.

For example, when disasters strike distant parts of the world, generous souls in other parts of the world, in deserts and lush meadows, on mountains and in valleys, on islands and continents, all contribute money to the persons afflicted. Millions of dollars to pay for assistance sometimes arrive at the disaster area within hours of the event.

In this case money is love in action—love which might be intended but could not be made effectual without the power of money as a medium of exchange.

Money serves as a unifying force and makes easier deeds of love, by which we can bestow on others the good things that they need.

Money Increases the Interdependence of Humans

The rich would have to eat money, but luckily the poor provide food.

Russian Proverb

Most of the time we think that the more money we have, the more independent we become. And there are certainly some senses in which this is true. Money allows us to buy homes the poor can't afford, drive cars the poor can't buy, travel where the poor can't go. In this sense, money does give us greater independence than the poor, but independence only in a limited way. For if we were truly independent, we wouldn't need money: we could provide for ourselves everything we need.

What about those homes we buy, the cars we drive, and the jets and ships that carry us to distant lands for our vacations? Can we construct those homes by ourselves, design and manufacture our cars, build and operate the ships and jets?

In fact, if other men and women chose not to build those homes, cars, jets, and ships, our money wouldn't give us more choices than the poor have. Were it not for the labors of tens of thousands of other souls who create the fine goods and provide the services we buy, our money would be worthless.

And even in societies where there's a vigorous economy making the good things we buy with our money, the value of our money depends on the character and stability of the segment of the culture we live in: "A dollar in a university is worth more than a dollar in a jail; in a temperate, schooled, law-abiding community, than in some sink of crime, where dice, knives, and arsenic, are in constant play."[76]

Money, which initially seems such a force for independence, is, on its deeper level, evidence that humans—particularly wealthy humans—need each other to make use of their money and to enjoy the good things money can buy.

Money, then, is a sign
of the interdependence of humans.

Money is evidence of how much we need each other just to get through the day. The very wealth which we often think frees us from the chains that grip others, binds us to those gripped by those chains. The value of our money depends on the character and efforts of tens of thousands of other persons, and the more money we spend, the more dependent we are on their character and efforts. Money, then, gives us more choices than those who lack it; but the more we spend, the more we must rely on others to provide the goods and services we buy.

Paradoxically, money gives us greater independence
while making us more dependent on others.

Wealth Should Be Valued by the Ends It Serves

> *Money never remains just coins and pieces of paper. Money can be translated into the beauty of living, a support in misfortune, an education, or future security. It also can be translated into a source of bitterness.*[77]

Sylvia Porter (1913–1991)

Some people seem to miss the deepest meaning of wealth, as in this pronouncement: "Money was never a big motivation for me, except as a way to keep score."[78] In what game and against whom? Even in using money to trumpet to the world their own success and importance, such folks affirm my point: the meaning of money lies not in itself, but in the ends it serves. Motivations such as this simply turn money to ends less significant than it's meant to serve; the fundamental meaning of wealth is still rooted in the fact that it eases the transfer of goods and services between persons.

At its core, money is a servant.

Now we judge a servant by two standards.

First, we say a servant is good if he performs his services discreetly and efficiently. In terms of efficiency, money is a good servant, which is why all successful cultures have some form of money; and it's why cultures which lack money fail to hold their own against cultures that do.

But we also judge servants by the ends they serve.

We lament the man who serves evil ends efficiently—the crafty thief and the clever forger. In our estimation, the evil ends they serve outweigh the fact that they serve those evil ends efficiently. It would be better, we know, for thieves and forgers not to be efficient than that they succeed in bringing about the evils they accomplish. A servant's greatest value arises from the values he serves.

And that's precisely what gives force to my friend's argument that

I ought to burn money that threatens to overthrow me or those I love. Better to destroy it than to let it do its evil work on us.

Now I said at the beginning of this inquiry that I would follow the evidence where it leads, but burning my money is a radical step, which I'm certainly not eager to take. So before we rest in my friend's conclusion, let's look a bit more closely at the nature of money, wealth, and property, to see if there's not some more palatable alternative.

◆ ◆ ◆

Unlike land, buildings, and other less liquid forms of wealth, money has no intrinsic value. On the contrary, "Money comes to life as it is spent."[79] This is one reason—but not the main reason—why money alone doesn't produce peace or happiness, or, in itself, even make a genuine contribution to an individual's fulfillment and sense of value. Wise souls—rich and poor—never forget that money is just a means to ends outside itself, and they remain vigilant against ever confusing their net worth with their self-worth.

Land, buildings, tools, and other non-liquid forms of wealth have some worth in themselves apart from their conventionally assigned or legal valuations. And in themselves, many of these assets can even enrich us spiritually simply because of what they are.

At sunset, the sight of a lovely lake nestled in a Georgia valley in the foothills of the Appalachians can lift the soul, as can the trim sailboat that scoots silently by, gliding over smooth, deep-green waters colored with reflections of clouds above.

A noble building, well designed and well built, can bring rest and comfort even to troubled souls. And there's even joy in simpler things well crafted: a sturdy shovel that feels good in the hands and digs the soil with ease and efficiency, or an ice-cream scoop that doesn't get clogged with ice cream. Just to work with such simple items brings happiness.

Doubtless, ownership of such things enriches the lives of those who own them. Strictly speaking, however, we don't have to own

that Georgia hillside or lake or sailboat or shovel to reap from them
practical and spiritual benefits: we only have to have the access to
them that is ordinarily granted by ownership. When you visit my
cottage and see the sunset I speak of, your soul will be lifted as much
as mine, even though you don't own what you see. Ownership is not
essential to the joy that fine things can bring us.[80]

Unlike money, these forms of wealth have value in themselves,
but their value is not inherently bound up with ownership of them;
their value exists apart from ownership. Ownership merely gives us
access to things like the lake or enables us to command the creation
of things like the cottage.

Which is why we prefer wealth to poverty.

◆ ◆ ◆

Now although such goods differ from money in that they have some
value in themselves, they remain like money in that their greatest
meaning lies not in what they are in themselves but in the values or
disvalues that we use them to serve.

In the scheme of things, a building used as a hospital in which
poor children are cured of cancer has greater real value than would
the same building if it were used as a laboratory that refines opium
into heroin for sale to addicts on the streets. Wealth used to establish and run the hospital is better used than wealth used to establish
and run the heroin lab. Essentially, then, wealth (like money) derives
its greatest significance from the ends it serves.

Wealth is meant to foster and protect
those things, activities, and values
that are true, good, and important in life.

These include things that rich and poor alike ought to treasure:
faith, family, friendship, community, honor, love, service, freedom,
and even beauty. These are the elements that are necessary if humans
are to flourish as they are meant to flourish. These are the values that

the wisest souls—rich and poor—have cherished throughout history, the values that you and I ought also to cherish and promote.
They ennoble souls; they're the foundation of just, generous, and enduring communities. And they're the highest purpose to which
wealth can be devoted.

It's not a matter of indifference whether you and I employ our
non-essential wealth in service of these ends or simply use it to indulge our whims and pleasures. When I use my wealth solely to pursue pleasure and delight, I set myself and my own interests above
others; I isolate myself from other men and women; I wound every
community of which I'm a member, including the most important
ones: marriage, family, and church. I wind up lonely and alone.

◆ ◆ ◆

The good news is that money is malleable.

In most cases, money that has long been directed to wrong ends
can be quickly redirected to better ones. For years we may have used
our money to indulge our appetites for high-quality goods and services, regardless of whether they're necessary or even *beneficial goods*.
We may even have become dependent upon and controlled by our
wealth and the power and pleasures it brings us. We may have lived
by the conviction that attainment of wealth is the critical measure of
our success and self-worth. And we may have pursued wealth obses-
sively and hoarded it anxiously, even as it brought us greater isolation and unhappiness.

No matter.

As I say, in terms of its ultimate value, money is malleable.

We can quickly redirect it away from bad ends to serve good ends;
we can rapidly conscript it into the service of the *fundamentals* that
promote our own genuine well-being—material, moral, and spiritual—and the well-being of others.

Such redemption of our money would be impossible if money
had within itself its primary meaning.

The redemption of wealth is blessedly possible
precisely because wealth derives its primary meaning
from the ends it serves.

Of course, it would be wrong to think that only the wealthy are tempted to use their money for improper ends. Not a person alive is exempt from this temptation: you struggle with it; I struggle with it. Every single day each one of us must seek to discover in the circumstances of that day the way in which we should use our money as a new occasion for redemption.

We must seek to employ our money in the service of values, not whims and pleasures. We must rule our money rather than letting it rule us. We must extract from it meaning and values that were not formerly there. By doing so, we add strength and goodness to the community in which we are members. We grow in love and wisdom and make it easier for others to do so, too.

The wise man subordinates his wealth to higher values, and so can we.

No.

He subordinates *himself* to higher values, and so can we.

By means of our money, we can become better persons, and we can make better persons of those who are close to us. The rest of this book is devoted to showing how.

PART II

WHAT YOUR MONEY CALLS YOU TO BE

chapter 8

non-essential wealth
is for the needy

That man is richest who, having perfected the functions
of his own life to the utmost, has also the widest helpful influence,
both personal, and by means of his possessions,
over the lives of others.[81]
—John Ruskin (1819–1900)

EARLIER, WE ESTABLISHED MEANS BY WHICH TO DETERMINE HOW MUCH OF OUR OWN WEALTH IS *NON-ESSENTIAL WEALTH* AND WE SAW THAT THERE ARE CERTAIN THINGS WE OUGHT NOT TO DO WITH IT. OUR CONSIDERATION OF THE CLASSICAL UNDERSTANDING OF PROPERTY AND THE UNIVERSAL DESTINATION OF GOODS SHOWED US THAT EVEN THOUGH WE HAVE AUTHORITY OVER IT, OUR *NON-ESSENTIAL WEALTH* IS NOT FULLY OURS TO DO WITH AS WE PLEASE. THE BOUNTY OF THE EARTH IS MEANT FOR THE WELL-BEING OF ALL:

*Any wealth we have beyond the fundamentals should be used
for the well-being of others, and specifically to provide the
fundamentals to those who lack them.*

Note that this classical argument does not claim that those of us
with money have an obligation to be charitable to the needy. We do
have that obligation; but a much more radical—even controver-
sial—point is being made here.

The universal destination of goods means that once you and I
have provided for our own *fundamentals* and the *fundamentals* of
those who depend on us, then—if others clearly and urgently need
our *non-essential wealth* for their own necessities—our *non-essential
wealth* in effect ceases to be ours to use for ourselves; we must use it
to serve the common good.

Yes, I said that in such circumstances, "our *non-essential wealth*
ceases to be ours to use for ourselves."

Put another way, the classical tradition says that if we have *non-
essential wealth* which another urgently needs for his own necessities,
then, to the extent that it's non-essential to us and indispensable to
him, that *non-essential wealth* is his to use. In other words, to possess
private property is not to possess the moral right to use that property in any way we please, but only as it is intended to be used. Our
non-essential wealth must be used, directly or indirectly, to benefit
those in need.[82]

◆ ◆ ◆

Vaudeville actress Sophie Tucker once said, "I've been rich and I've
been poor: rich is better."[83]

No kidding!

Conclusions like the one we just reached a few paragraphs ago
threaten to make you and me poor again, and I don't like that one
bit. Plus, I'm neither a socialist nor a communist. I believe that the
market economy and private property can be instruments of virtue.

But perhaps giving away all our wealth now is not a necessary consequence of these arguments. So before you put this book down and go elsewhere, bear with me for a few more pages. I've got a lot of *non-essential wealth*, and when I first saw this consequence of the points made so far in this book, I was a little agitated.

I have some responses to this unsettling conclusion, and, having walked this far down the path with me, it's probably better that you continue walking than that you stop here. If you turn away now, I can't help you come to the resolution of this problem that I think retains the truth in what we have said about the universal destination of goods while modulating it with other truths that show that it's not merely palatable, but can even be a surprising opportunity for those of us who have a considerable amount of *non-essential wealth*.

So bear with me for a few more pages.

◆ ◆ ◆

But before you do, fasten your seatbelt, because there's one more unpleasant argument we have to hear before we turn to solutions. It's a strong claim, made even more formidable by the fact that it's made not by some college kid who's just discovered Marx, ethics, and economics, but by a canonized saint, a man of experience and prayer who's wise in the ways of justice and the ways of the world.

If we're to get to the bottom of all this, if we're finally to give to our wealth the answers it demands, then we have to hear the strongest arguments that can be brought forth.

Only after that's done will it make sense to take up the task of discovering that response which is true and right for each of us in our own unique circumstances.

◆ ◆ ◆

Forewarned, then, let's turn directly to the most unpalatable conclusion that follows from the universal destination of goods and the classical notion of property that even our government accepts: because the goods of the earth were provided for the well-being of all men and women, then once we have secured the *fundamentals* for ourselves and that of our dependents, anything left over may continue legally to be ours, but it's not for our use: it's meant to provide for the common good.

Put another way, when we fail to use our *non-essential wealth* to provide for the common good, we're not acting uncharitably; we're withholding from others goods that are theirs by virtue of their neediness and the universal destination of goods.

To drive this point home, Aquinas quotes the frightening words of St. Ambrose, the harshest charge that's ever been leveled against me and my wealth by someone I respect, and the harshest charge that's likely to be leveled against you and your wealth by someone you should respect.

According to St. Ambrose, when you hold on to your *non-essential wealth*,

> It is the hungry man's bread that you withhold, the naked man's cloak you store away. The money you bury in the earth is the price of the poor man's ransom and freedom.[84]

Now I could respond to St. Ambrose that I haven't buried any of my *non-essential wealth*. Burying it might have been reasonable in the feudal society in which he lived, but in our vigorous capitalist economy, burying money would be foolish. I've invested my *non-essential wealth*. It's not idle. I'm working it diligently to earn a good return on it.

That's irrelevant, St. Ambrose could argue. That wealth is still mine. I haven't given the greater part of it to the hungry and needy.

Is it then the hungry man's bread that I withhold? The naked man's cloak that I store away?

When I encountered St. Ambrose's comments about wealth, I felt with new force Jesus' words, "It's easier for a camel to pass through the eye of a needle than for a rich man to enter the kingdom of Heaven,"[85] and I grew concerned.

chapter 9

virtue: the first vocation
of those with money

There is no greater wealth than virtue,
and no greater loss than to forget it.[86]
—Tiruvalluvar (5th century A.D.)

IN THE SIXTIES IT WAS FASHIONABLE TO SPEAK OF FOLKS LIKE ME AS "CAPITALIST PIGS," AND TO SCORN MONEY AND BUSINESS. EVEN TODAY OUR CULTURE IS TAINTED BY THE WIDESPREAD ASSUMPTION THAT THOSE OF US WHO HAVE SUCCEEDED IN BUSINESS HAVE DONE SO BY IMMORAL OR ILLICIT PRACTICES, AND THAT WE'RE WILLING TO USE ANY MEANS WHATSOEVER TO MAKE MONEY.

According to this line of thinking, ethics simply doesn't concern us capitalist pigs.

Now although there are some ruthless businessmen out there who fit this stereotype, my experience is that the great majority of businessmen are honorable civic-minded people who genuinely want to know what's right and to do it.

They seek not simply to be good businessmen and women, but to be good men and women simply.

Indeed, although cheating may make a quick buck and exploiting customers may win profits short term, I'm convinced that the long-term financial value of a company depends on its other values—and specifically on its moral values. Honest, hardworking men and women make the best employees, the best employers, and the most successful businesspeople. They contribute the most to their communities, fiscally and morally.

For years now, in my own life and despite my many failures, I've sought not only to be an honest, hardworking businessman; I've wanted to reach higher—to discern the will of God for me and to live in accordance with His will, especially insofar as my wealth concerns the will of God.

In reaching higher, I'm not really doing anything extraordinary.

I'm merely aspiring to the goal that animates all men and women of goodwill, all serious Christians, and believers in many other religions. As persons, and regardless of our state in life, we seek not to live for ourselves, but to acknowledge our Creator and to do that which we believe He put us on this earth to do. In almost all faiths, a life in accordance with the will of God, a life of virtue, is known as "holiness," and although I'm not anywhere near achieving holiness, I do desire it.

A virtuous life in accordance with God's will is the primary vocation of every person, from the poorest of the poor to the wealthiest among us, and all those in between. Man, woman, white, black, young, old, tall, short: each of us is called to discover the particular will of God for us individually—what some folks call our "personal vocation"; and our virtue consists in living in accordance with it.[87]

Even atheists have an inkling of this singular calling when they catalog their talents, desires, and opportunities, consider the needs of those around them, and decide that *this* is what they are called to do with their lives.

Called to do with their lives.

Meant to do with them.

Not as one option out of many which happens to strike their fancy, but as the life-calling which constitutes the meaning of their lives.

In this way, without acknowledging the existence of God, even atheists are able to find in the elements of their lives the special summons that God has given them, the task that is uniquely theirs for their time on earth: their vocation.

◆ ◆ ◆

If we fail in this vocation to be holy, then, it seems to me, it doesn't matter how great our wealth may be, or how crippling our poverty: we've missed our fundamental vocation and failed at the most important task that was given us.

Because virtue in this sense is the primary vocation
of every living human being, it is also
the primary vocation of the wealthy.

◆ ◆ ◆

Which is why, as I mentioned earlier, I was so troubled when I discovered the universal destination of goods and saw how it leads to St. Ambrose's denunciation of those of us who use our *non-essential wealth* on ourselves: "It is the hungry man's bread that you withhold, the naked man's cloak you store away. The money you bury in the earth is the price of the poor man's ransom and freedom."

When I read that I paused, considered the enormity of my own *non-essential wealth,* . . . and grew concerned. For when a man with a little *non-essential wealth* fails to devote it to the needy, he deprives the poor of only a few loaves and keeps a cloak from only a few souls huddling in the rain and the cold.

But me?

How many millions of loaves has my wealth kept from the poor?

How many tens of thousands of souls have shivered in the rain because they were denied money I have but don't need for my *fundamentals?*

When I became convinced of the universal destination of goods and saw the force of the demands it places on me as a wealthy person, I was tempted to stop thinking about my money, to close my eyes to what I'd come to understand, even to abandon my practice of seeking truth and virtue, no matter how painful.

How can it be true that I have to give up almost everything I have?

Everything I've earned?

Must I really give away all of my *non-essential wealth?*

◆ ◆ ◆

At this point, it's important to remember that the arguments I've made so far in this book are philosophical, not theological: they're based on reason and are rooted in the common sense of mankind these past twenty-five hundred years. In these pages, we've moved from the classical understanding of the nature of property to recognition of the universal destination of goods. There's no religion in that progression.

What shakes me as a Christian is that the philosophical arguments I've discovered in the course of these investigations echo the words of Jesus to the rich young man:

> Jesus said unto him, "If thou wilt be perfect, go and sell what thou hast, and give it to the poor, and thou shalt have treasure in heaven: and come and follow me." But when the young man heard that saying, he went away sorrowful: for he had great possessions. Then said Jesus unto his disciples, "Verily I say unto you, That a rich man shall hardly enter into the kingdom of heaven. And again I say unto you, It is easier for a camel to go through the eye of a needle, than for a rich man to enter into the kingdom of God." When his disciples heard it,

they were exceedingly amazed, saying, "Who then can be saved?"[88]

◆ ◆ ◆

One of my philosopher friends says that whenever he encounters questions like this whose answers seem so counterintuitive, he never commits himself to an answer right away but looks to see if there's a crucial point that's been overlooked, a distinction that can make better sense out of the evidence and satisfy the competing claims equitably.

I want to do what's right.

I even want to do the will of God.

But I'm still relatively young, and I don't really want to give up the *non-essential wealth* I've worked so hard to get and that I believe I can increase if only I'm allowed to keep it.

Do the nature of property and the universal destination of goods really compel me to give all my *non-essential wealth* away, and you to do the same?

◆ ◆ ◆

After getting over the shock of the possible implications of the universal destination of goods, I realized that I'd overlooked the critical distinction between *ownership* and *use*. As a result, I'd grown fearful of an answer that's more devastating to me than the evidence can justify.

It's true that our consideration of the nature of property led us to conclude that we must use our *non-essential wealth* for those who lack the *fundamentals*. That conclusion, however, doesn't address the question of whether *using* our *non-essential wealth* for those who lack the *fundamentals* means we must cease to *own* our *non-essential wealth*.

There may be ways we can retain ownership of our *non-essential wealth* while living in accordance with the ethical demands implicit

"You can't sleep well, Mr. Siskin? You—a rich man?"

in its ownership and the universal destination of goods. Indeed, some persons may even be morally obliged to retain ownership of their *non-essential wealth* in order both to ensure that in the present it's used for the benefit of many and that, in years to come, through their successes in increasing it, there's yet more to be used for those who lack the *fundamentals*.

In a word, there may be, for some of us at least, ways in which our *non-essential wealth* does not conflict with our primary vocation to be virtuous and do the will of God. There may, in fact, be ways in which our *non-essential wealth* is an essential element in the particular, individual task that has been laid before us as the unique calling and meaning of each of our lives. This was John D. Rockefeller's understanding of wealth and the one whose implications we shall explore in the coming pages:

> How is it consistent with the universal diffusion of these blessings that vast sums of money should be in single hands? The reply is, as I see it, that, while men of wealth control great sums of money, they do not and cannot use them for themselves. They have, indeed, the legal title to large properties, and they do control the investment of them, but that is as far as their own relation to them extends.[89]

Without undermining what we've discovered about the nature of property and the universal destination of goods, Rockefeller's formulation of the meaning of wealth suggests that the complete answer to the question of what we must do with our *non-essential wealth* may be both less threatening than the words of St. Ambrose, and more hopeful and more consoling.

Indeed, the truth finally brings us to a spiritually liberating understanding of the meaning of our wealth and provides sure guidelines by which to determine just how we should employ it. For many of us, managing our wealth to bring about the universal destination of goods may be the path to virtue: the way that we, in particular, fulfill the will of God for our individual lives.

chapter 10

wealth creation:
the second vocation
of those with money

You cannot strengthen the weak by weakening the strong.
You cannot help the wage earner by pulling down the wage payer.
You cannot help the poor by destroying the rich.[90]
—William Henry Boetcker (1873–1962)

I'VE ALWAYS THOUGHT THAT THERE ARE REALLY ONLY FOUR WAYS TO GET MONEY: YOU CAN STEAL IT; YOU CAN WIN IT GAMBLING; YOU CAN RECEIVE IT AS A GIFT OR INHERITANCE; OR YOU CAN CREATE IT. THE FIRST THREE WAYS ARE ZERO-SUM GAMES: MONEY MOVES FROM ONE PERSON'S POCKET TO ANOTHER'S; ONE PERSON GETS RICHER BECAUSE THE OTHER GETS POORER.

The fourth way—wealth creation—does more than bring in money by transferring it from your pocket to mine. It increases the amount of wealth in the world, so that everyone winds up better off financially.

For example, a company that builds cheaper, more fuel-efficient automobile engines and sells them to Detroit earns money from those sales; Detroit increases sales and earnings by selling more cars because consumers want fuel efficiency; and the car buyers wind up with more money in their pockets because they save money on gasoline every mile they drive. At the end of the day, everyone involved is better off financially.

Isn't this the case with most businesses?

They begin with material and immaterial goods as raw material and—in various ways, directly and indirectly—draw forth from that raw material goods and services that would otherwise not have been available. And they do that in such a way that all who are involved with the process—from owners to workers to consumers—are enriched by the existence of those businesses and their involvement with those businesses; all grow wealthier or are in some way better off from the activities of those businesses. In a word, these businesses create wealth. They help ensure that the goods of the earth reach those persons for whom they are, by nature, destined.

Emerson captured vividly the benefits to society of wealth creation:

> Wealth begins in a tight roof that keeps the rain and wind out; in a good pump that yields you plenty of sweet water; in two suits of clothes, so to change your dress when you are wet; in dry sticks to burn; in a good double-wick lamp; and three meals; in a horse, or a locomotive, to cross the land; in a boat to cross the sea; in tools to work with; in books to read; and so, in giving, on all sides, by tools and auxiliaries, the greatest possible extension to our powers, as if it added feet, and hands, and eyes, and blood, length to the day, and knowledge, and good-will.*

---

* Emerson, "Wealth." Not only does wealth creation benefit all men, it tends to draw the resources of the earth under the control of those who are most able to use them to create greater wealth, and most intent on doing so. As Emerson says elsewhere in this same essay, "Open the doors of opportunity to talent and

136 ◆ what your money means

Wealth Creation Serves the Universal Destination of Goods

When such visionary activities are wedded to labor, capital, and perseverance, the whole world is lifted; rich and poor benefit, and continue to benefit for many years. No wonder some people argue that wealth creation as I have just described it helps the poor more than do alms: "You are much surer that you are doing good when you pay money to those who work, as the recompense of their labor, than when you give money merely in charity."[91]

Or, as John D. Rockefeller noted a century ago,

> The best philanthropy, the help that does the most good and the least harm, the help that nourishes civilization at its very root, that most widely disseminates health, righteousness, and happiness, is not what is usually called charity. It is, in my judgment, the investment of effort or time or money, carefully considered with relation to the power of employing people at a remunerative wage, to expand and develop the resources at hand, and to give opportunity for progress and healthful labor where it did not exist before. No mere money-giving is comparable to this in its lasting and beneficial results.[92]

Now some persons might argue that only businesses that produce the *fundamentals* truly create wealth. By this measure, companies that create low-cost power generators for third-world countries are wealth creators; those that produce frivolous items like the tacky plastic toys in Cracker Jack boxes aren't.

Surely we're better off when both a company's existence and its

virtue, and they will do themselves justice, and property will not be in bad hands. In a free and just commonwealth, property rushes from the idle and imbecile, to the industrious, brave, and persevering."

products create wealth, providing the *fundamentals* to those who work there and offering helpful products to those who buy what the factory makes or the service it renders. But that's not always possible. In the fifties, "Made in Japan" was synonymous with "junk," as thousands of Japanese factories lifted Japan out of war-induced poverty by creating for the American market millions of tacky toys little better than the toys in Cracker Jack boxes today. Many a birthday kid threw away the Japanese cap gun that broke just minutes after he blew out the candles and opened the package that contained it.

The poet Richard Wilbur denounced the makers of such goods in his delightful poem entitled "Junk":

> Haul them off! Hide them!
> The heart winces
> For junk and gimcrack,
> For jerrybuilt things
> And the men who make them
> For a little money. . . .[93]

I don't defend the creation and sale of such junk. I use the example to indicate that although the products of such factories were shoddy, those factories did employ millions of Japanese workers, providing the *fundamentals* to millions of souls who otherwise would have remained destitute.

On the backs of such shoddy products was built modern Japan, the economic powerhouse that, just thirty years after its devastation in World War II, was one of the wealthiest countries in the world. Those doodads may not have been well crafted or durable, but they did the Japanese an essential service and, by means of wealth creation, they fulfilled the mandate that, nine hundred years ago, Maimonides gave us: "Anticipate charity by preventing poverty."[94]

So although it's better when businesses produce significant goods and services, even those that create and distribute frivolous things are helping to bring about the universal destination of goods insofar as, by means of salaries and benefits, they provide the *fundamentals* to their workers.

Nor should we underestimate the benefit that comes from having honorable employment, particularly when that employment relies on a person's talents, skills, and abilities. These things each help workers, managers, and owners flourish as human beings. Indeed, the best businesses enrich everyone who is associated with them in any way: the owner, workers, managers, and those who employ the products or services provided by these businesses.[95]

In a word, it's better that such businesses exist than that they not exist.*

◆ ◆ ◆

At this point, it's not difficult for me to accept Aristotle's point that "Wealth as a whole consists in using things rather than in owning them; it's really the activity—that is, the use—of property that constitutes wealth."[96]

But is the use of my wealth in my businesses compatible with St. Ambrose's charge that when we fail to use our *non-essential wealth* for those who lack the *bare necessities* or who can't fulfill their *gen-*

---

* Of course, it's wrong to establish and run a business that gravely harms those who work there, as was often the case in past centuries when workers were seen literally to be expendable and employers did nothing to ensure that workplaces were safe environments in which workers could flourish. And that's why it's wrong to establish and run businesses whose products or services debase those who use them: it would never be licit to engage in the production and sale of heroin or pornography, the running of a prostitution ring, or the buying and selling of human slaves.

Businesses that corrupt or debase others serve their owners but harm others who have contact with them. Such businesses sometimes make their owners wealthy, and are even engaged in by some who are already wealthy, but they don't help bring about the universal destination of goods.

uine needs, we deprive the hungry man of bread and the naked man of a cloak?

Must we simply give all of our *non-essential wealth* to the poor? Perhaps not.

Among the many parables of Jesus is a surprising one in the book of Matthew.[97] There Jesus tells of a master who goes away for some time, dividing among three of his servants some funds that he is leaving with them for safekeeping. One servant buries the money, and, when his master comes back, returns to him the exact amount that the master placed in his hands for safekeeping. The other two servants invest the funds left with them, increasing their master's money while he was away.

In Jesus' parable, the master sharply rebukes the servant who buries the money, saying that if the servant wasn't willing to use it to make more money, he ought at least to have invested it with bankers so that when the master returned, he would have more money to work with.

Jesus' parable puts St. Ambrose's comment in a new light, and helps us understand better the relation we ought to have to the *non-essential wealth* over which we have control.

For Jesus and St. Ambrose both condemn burying the money, leaving it idle. Whether it be given directly to the poor or put to work to earn more that can later be used for the common good, they insist that *non-essential wealth* not be idle.

What does that mean for you and me?

What if you and I retain control of our *non-essential wealth* but don't spend it on ourselves or simply hold on to it? What if we employ it in wealth-generating businesses, businesses that, like many technology companies, don't only earn money, but create wealth as we have explained it, improving the lot of everyone whose lives their efforts and products touch?

Rather than depriving the hungry of bread and the naked of cloaks, businesses so ordered multiply the loaves of bread available and lower their cost; they increase the number of cloaks available and make them so cheap that even the very poor can afford to be warmed by them for years to come.*

Might that not be a use of our *non-essential wealth* that's better than simply giving it outright to those who lack the *fundamentals?* If so, then, we ought not hasten to get free of our *non-essential wealth*, but rather we should seek ways to employ it so that it helps to bring about the universal destination of goods.

Hillaire Belloc captured this duty humorously but exactly:

> Lord Finchley tried to mend the Electric Light
> Himself. It struck him dead: And serve him right!
> It is the business of the wealthy man
> To give employment to the artisan.[98]

Some People Have a Vocation to Create Wealth

> *I believe the power to make money is a gift from God . . . to be developed and used to the best of our ability for the good of mankind. Having been endowed with the gift I possess, I believe it is my duty to make money and still more money and to use the money I make for the good of my fellow man according to the dictates of my conscience.*[99]

> John D. Rockefeller (1839–1937)

I'm convinced that each one of us has a special vocation we're called to fulfill in this life, a unique work that is ours alone and that makes us indispensable in the universal scheme of things.

---

* Grisez, *Living a Christian Life,* 814: "Sometimes, although its owners could give away property or money, they have such a gift for administering material goods that they should accept that as an element of their personal vocation. For example, people with both surplus wealth and skill in management can rightly set up or invest in businesses which provide just wages for gainful work and useful goods and services at fair prices, along with enough profit to compensate them reasonably for their work, which contributes to society's economic common good."

In this time and in this place, no one else is called to do quite what I am called to do: be the husband of my wife, the father of my daughter, and the steward of my resources. No one else is called to do quite what I'm called to do; nor can I be replaced in the doing of these things. In this sense, each one of us is not merely important, but indispensable; and each one of us is called to discover the particular, unique ways in which we are indispensable. I believe that this notion is more than sentimentality. It's rooted in who I am and who you are, physically as well as mentally.

You see, there's not really much that we receive at birth that's random or meaningless. We're born with an eye composed of many parts—lens, cornea, iris, retina—that work together with incredible efficiency to give us sight near and far, in light bright and dim. Are the parts of the eye arrayed randomly? Is their organization meaningless?

No. They're well ordered to a specific end—sight—which provides us the means to find food for our body, avoid dangers, and delight in the things of creation.

And our digestive system: it's composed of many parts—tongue, teeth, stomach, gall bladder, small and large intestines, and countless other lesser parts and chemical processes that work together with great efficiency to extract energy from vegetables and meat, from foods cooked and raw.

Are the parts of our digestive system arrayed randomly?

Is their organization meaningless or are they ordered to a definitive end—digestion—which provides food for our entire body from birth to death?

No matter what biologists study in the body, they find that the parts are intricately designed to serve the whole of human life. And if biologists can't immediately discover that purpose, they search until they do. Biologists wouldn't sustain that search for years (and sometimes even decades) if they thought that the physical elements that constitute the human body were just a conglomeration of random parts. By their actions in seeking the meaning and purpose of the parts of living things, even nihilistic scientists testify that they're convinced that the body has been ordered marvelously and well formed.

Our minds, too, manifest the same remarkable organization: they grasp the meaning of what we see and hear; they enable us to walk without falling, to drive at high speed on crowded freeways, to form words and to understand the things said to us. Memory liberates us from the tyranny of the present, enabling us to face today's threats armed with wisdom gleaned from yesterday's experiences. Understanding discovers trends that allow us to foresee what's likely to happen tomorrow; free will enables us to shape the future as we desire, which is how we create wealth.

Just as there's nothing random and meaningless about the organization and functioning of the physical parts of our bodies, so there's nothing random or meaningless about the organization and functioning of the powers of our minds.

◆ ◆ ◆

Now what about our energy and our intelligence, and especially our talent for identifying opportunities and gathering the resources and talent necessary to transform those opportunities into products and services that have value for many people?

What are we supposed to make of our ability to create wealth?

In a creature as well crafted as the human person, with every part and activity, mental and physical, working together to serve definite purposes, these capacities or talents are in no way random.

If we have a knack for creating wealth, it is not a meaningless part of who we are, an element of our soul that we can ignore as irrelevant in determining what we're called to do in this life.

Author Vida Scudder remarked that "It is through creating, not possessing, that life is revealed."[100] It is through creating, not possessing, that you and I reveal who we are.

Indeed, it is through creating, not possessing, that we make ourselves who we are, that we give to our lives that meaning which it is

our calling to give—and we are talking here not merely about artistic creation, but even the creation of wealth.

In fact, the ability to create wealth has considerable meaning, and is a major factor that must be taken into account when deciding what we should do with our *non-essential wealth* as we seek to help to bring about the universal destination of goods.

◆ ◆ ◆

You and I may have never felt called to anything like the ministry or medicine. But we might have a pretty good knack for creating wealth. Don't misunderstand me. I don't mean that business is the purpose of our lives in any absolute sense; I just mean that in the same way you can conclude that the eye is meant to see and the digestive system to provide energy, so, I think, it may be right to conclude that our talent for creating wealth is meant to play a significant role in our lives, and shouldn't simply be dismissed as meaningless, or, as some would do, disparaged as money-grubbing, wrong, or evil—so long as we never confuse our talent with its purpose.

We said already that the eye doesn't see for itself, but for the person whose eye it is. Seeing is for understanding, not simply for seeing. And the digestive system doesn't provide energy only or primarily for itself, but for the person whose digestive system it is: digesting is for energy for the whole body—for life, and not simply for itself.

In the same way, a knack for making money is not for itself, but for a purpose higher than itself and outside of itself. Specifically, the creation of wealth can, in fact, be a vocation, and so long as we can continue to create wealth efficiently, we have a general obligation to do so—not, to be sure, solely so our own assets can increase, but so that through our efforts others may obtain the *fundamentals* and we may help to serve the universal destination of goods.

◆ ◆ ◆

Initially it may sound odd to speak of wealth creation as a vocation. Usually we restrict the term "vocation" to selfless professions like medicine and the ministry, or we broaden the term to include the fundamental calling we have in life: marriage is ordinarily understood as a vocation, as is the priesthood, which are both fundamental, lifelong choices about our state in life, choices which involve the complete and irrevocable gift of self to others. Insofar as they contain within themselves a similar, if not lifelong, call to selflessness—particularly in service to other individuals—teaching and medicine can also be seen to be vocations. It seems to me that

> *Understood correctly and chosen as an act of service, wealth*
> *creation can be as much a vocation as teaching*
> *or being a doctor.*

◆ ◆ ◆

Does everyone who comes into wealth thereby inherit the vocation to create wealth?

That would be absurd.

Speaking in her autobiography about her lack of business acumen, Margaret C. Anderson says, "I can't earn my own living. I could never make anything turn into money. It's like making fires. A careful assortment of paper, shavings, faggots and kindling nicely tipped with pitch will never light for me. I have never been present when a cigarette butt, extinct, thrown into a damp and isolated spot, started a conflagration in the California woods."[101]

Anderson is the antithesis of someone with a vocation for wealth creation. Were she to inherit ten million dollars, her attempts to use it herself would likely lead to the quick dissipation of her inheritance in ill-considered efforts.

> *The having of money is not sufficient evidence*
> *that a person has a vocation to create wealth.*

It takes, as I have described above, that special group of skills and interests as a knack for making money.

If you've been in business a while and have succeeded in many of the businesses you've engaged in, then it's likely that, for the moment at least, you have that vocation. If, however, most of your

"Well, yes we've put your money to work.
As for what it's doing at this very moment, I have no idea."

business decisions prove faulty or bring little real fruit, then probably you don't have this particular vocation. In that case, it could be wrong for you to risk your *non-essential wealth* by attempting, without the requisite talent or skills, to increase it. Rather than increasing the wealth available in the world and helping to realize the universal destination of goods, you might just wind up transferring that wealth into the hands of a few selfish or unscrupulous persons who will use it for themselves.

Because our *non-essential wealth* is not for ourselves, if you don't have a knack for creating wealth (as I have explained it here), then there are other things you must do with your *non-essential wealth*, and it could in fact be imprudent for you to try to create wealth with it.

> *Regardless of your particular personal vocation,*
> *you must use your non-essential wealth to bring about*
> *the universal destination of goods.*

What, then, must we do when we find ourselves with *non-essential wealth* that's not being used to provide the *fundamentals* to others? Neither our lack of interest in engaging in activities that create wealth for others nor our lack of aptitude for doing so exempt us from the obligation to ensure that our *non-essential wealth* gets used for the purpose for which it was originally given to mankind: to provide the *fundamentals* for all.

If we can't use our *non-essential wealth* for that purpose, then we've got to get it into the hands of those who can and will.

◆ ◆ ◆

For the moment, however, our topic is not those who lack the vocation to create wealth, it's those who have that vocation.

What about you? Do your decisions continue to cause your businesses to flourish and the investments you make to increase in value? Is your net worth increasing so you can employ your earnings to grow your businesses and to establish new ones?

If so, then there's a good chance that you are someone called by

God as one of His instruments by which He seeks to gather and organize the raw resources of the earth—material and non-material—in order to make them available to those who lack the *fundamentals* and cannot gather the *fundamentals* for themselves alone.

You have the vocation to create wealth for the good of all.

That's the meaning and purpose of *non-essential wealth*.

That's the answer to what we should do with it (and with our lives).

We're called to be stewards of creation, to ensure that, to the extent that we have ownership or authority over them, the goods of the earth needed by the poor don't lie fallow, don't get squandered, don't get used inefficiently, and don't get diverted to the private use of a few individuals whose *fundamentals* are already secured.

In many respects, our *non-essential wealth* is akin to money that has been placed into the hands of a venture capitalist. Although he has control over it, that wealth doesn't belong to the venture capitalist: he's charged only with working that money to yield the greatest return for his investors.

In a similar way, we control the goods of the earth that constitute our *non-essential wealth*, but like the venture capitalist we mustn't use those goods solely for ourselves. We must use them to yield the greatest return for those whom we are called to serve.

Now it would be wrong for a venture capitalist to squander the funds that have been entrusted to him or to destroy them. In the same way, if we have a vocation to create wealth, it would be wrong for us to squander our *non-essential wealth* or to destroy it.

> *That we have non-essential wealth is no accident: it was given
> to us—or we were allowed to earn it—for a reason:
> so that, as good stewards, we can use it for others.*

◆ ◆ ◆

We have before us now the elements of a solution, a solution which encompasses all that we've learned about the need of all persons for the *fundamentals*, the dangers of *non-essential wealth* to ourselves and others, the meaning of money and wealth, the universal destination of goods, the nature and purpose of ownership, and even the unique vocation that some of us may have to create wealth. And that solution is, really, simple:

> *If we have a vocation to create wealth, then, so long*
> *as we're capable of engaging in that vocation and willing*
> *to do so, it's licit for us to retain control over some portion of*
> *our non-essential wealth in order to use it to create new wealth*
> *that will help bring about the ends called for by the*
> *universal destination of goods.*

So long as we do this, we're not, as St. Ambrose charged, stealing bread from the mouths of the hungry or taking from those who are cold the cloaks they need for warmth.

On the contrary, with our God-given talents, with our money, our other material goods, and with our psychological, intellectual, and spiritual wealth we're serving them by creating in this world more bread and more cloaks, and ensuring that bread and cloaks get to the souls who need them most.

St. Basil summarized it this way:

> Why are you rich while another is poor, unless it be that you
> may have the merit of good stewardship and he (the poor man)
> the reward of patience?[102]

What we have found is a solution to the problem of wealth for those whose vocation is the creation of wealth—a solution that St. Ambrose would not merely find acceptable, but surely would applaud.

The Meaning and Value of the Vocation to Create Wealth

Some men are born to own, and can animate all their possessions. Others cannot: their owning is not graceful; seems to be a compromise of their character: they seem to steal their own dividends. They should own who can administer; not they who hoard and conceal; not they who, the greater proprietors they are, are only the greater beggars, but they whose work carves out work for more, opens a path for all.[103]

Ralph Waldo Emerson (1803–1882)

Wise souls see their *non-essential wealth* as an instrument that must be used to provide the *fundamentals* to those who lack them. They subordinate themselves and their *non-essential wealth* to goods greater than self and money. By choosing the path of service, they

"My summer vacation: How I made money in a bear market."

grow in humility; they ennoble themselves; and they render themselves less vulnerable to the corrupting powers of wealth. They also understand that

If we have a vocation to create wealth,
it's not because of any merit of our own.

Atheists might say that a person with a talent for creating wealth just happened to be born with those interests and skills; I say that God gave them to him. Regardless of the source to which you ascribe the vocation to create wealth, you usually can't convincingly ascribe it to the person himself, for no one gives himself his own talents.

Some people find themselves with an interest in music and a knack for learning instruments and playing them well; some people find themselves with an interest in teaching, and a knack for doing it well.

I believe that such a talent for music or teaching is both a gift and a calling. Those who receive the gifts of these talents are singled out to serve others by means of the talents that were given to them.

When I was younger—and without having chosen it—I found myself with an interest in creating wealth and a talent for doing it. Just as those with a gift for music or teaching are singled out and called to use their gifts for others, so I believe that I've been singled out to use my talents to help provide the *fundamentals* to others by the creation of wealth.

If you, also, have a talent for creating or amassing wealth, then you, too, have been given a gift and a calling you should use to help provide the *fundamentals* to others.

Now whereas some might suggest that having a talent for music or teaching or wealth creation is a reason for pride, I consider each one a privilege and a responsibility which should be approached with fear and trembling.

Modest circumstances limit the impact that most souls can have in this life, restricting their influence and impact to a few; but wealth (and, certainly, significant wealth) places in our hands the well-being of many souls.

> *It's a privilege to be called to the noble work*
> *of the wealthy, but it's also a heavy responsibility*
> *not easily fulfilled.*

Fear and trembling?

Yes, because, as we saw, *non-essential wealth* affords us so many occasions to fall into self-indulgence or, when we're less recollected, to wield our wealth as a weapon to force others to do our bidding, even while undertaking work that may be, in itself, noble and good.

Having experienced the temptations that accompany wealth as we use our talents to seek to do good, Andrew Carnegie called those who are wealthy to a kind of austerity that is calculated to keep their motives pure:

> This then is held to be the duty of the man of wealth: To set an example of modest, unostentatious living, shunning display or extravagance; to provide moderately for the legitimate wants of those dependent on him; and, after doing so, to consider all surplus revenues which come to him simply as trust funds, which he is called upon to administer, and strictly bound as a matter of duty to administer in the manner which in his judgment is best calculated to produce the most beneficial results for the community—the man of wealth thus becoming the mere trustee and agent for his poorer brethren, bringing to their service his superior wisdom, experience, and ability to administer, doing for them better than they could or would do for themselves.[104]

To ensure that I continue to live in accordance with this high call enunciated by Carnegie, I strive always to awaken and keep alive in my soul the virtues of public-spiritedness, honesty, humility, fairness, and temperance. I strive always to remind myself, even in the midst of the most intense business deals, when millions of dollars are at stake, that I'm simply a steward, and that I have my wealth so I may use it to meet genuine human needs fairly and efficiently.

I recall that old woman with her potato, and I remember that, in a very real sense, I am she and she is me: the difference in size between her wealth and mine is essentially irrelevant. What matters is the soul: whether her attitude and actions regarding her potato enrich or impoverish her soul; and whether my attitudes and actions regarding my money enrich or impoverish mine.

chapter 11

giving: the third vocation
of those with money

Riches are for spending,
and spending for honor and good actions.[105]
—Sir Francis Bacon (1561–1626)

UNLIKE OTHER LIFELONG VOCATIONS, THE VOCATION TO CREATE WEALTH CAN BE MORE FLEETING. THE PERSON CONCERNED WITH HELPING TO BRING ABOUT THE UNIVERSAL DESTINATION OF GOODS MUST REMAIN EVER CONSCIOUS THAT AT SOME POINT THAT VOCATION MAY NO LONGER BE HIS.

Speaking of show business, Irving Berlin once said that "The toughest thing about success is that you've got to keep on being a success. Talent is only a starting point in this business. You've got to keep on working that talent. Someday I'll reach for it and it won't be there."[106]

The same is true in my line.

As a creator of wealth, some day I'm going to lose my edge. My love of business may wane, my keenness in following the markets may grow dull, my attention may drift toward other interests. Those changes in me will quickly erode my ability to create more wealth from what I have already. If I'm not careful, they may even cause my wealth to start declining and the good done for others through my businesses to diminish.

Two hundred fifty years ago, in his poem "The Deserted Village," Irish poet Oliver Goldsmith said, "Ill fares the land, to hastening ills a prey, / Where wealth accumulates, and men decay."[107] Goldsmith's concern was the destruction of the peasantry, but, especially these days, a country fares equally ill when its wealth creators decay—when you and I lose our edge.

When that happens to me, my relation to my *non-essential wealth* will become like that of a person without business sense or experience who inherits millions. I'll have to adopt different tactics to ensure that my wealth is used to help bring about the universal destination of goods. To fulfill my vocational responsibility to use my *non-essential wealth* to bring about the universal destination of goods, I'll have to transfer my non-productive *non-essential wealth* to others who can use it for that end better than I can.

For me and for you, such a transfer is a responsibility that springs from the fact that although some of us are allowed to own it for a time, we are to use our property to serve the well-being of others also and we must ensure that while we own it, it serves that end.

Later we'll consider a way to make such transfers in ways that not only help bring about the universal destination of goods, but even shield from the dangers of *non-essential wealth* those who are close to us and, finally, even serve for them as a school of virtue.[108]

Although we may only be obligated to transfer our *non-essential wealth* to others when we cease to use it for wealth creation, there are a number of very good prudential reasons to begin transferring at least some of it to others *before* we reach the point where we can ourselves no longer create new wealth with it.

Giving Now Saves Those Who Can't Afford to Wait until Tomorrow

A gift in season is a double favor to the needy.

Publilius Syrus (1st century B.C.)

In his book *Wealthy and Wise*, Claude Rosenberg Jr. challenges those of us who are tempted to hold on to all of our money now so that we may increase earnings and give away more later: "What are the expenses we incur by delaying cures for deadly diseases? Who can calculate the costs to individuals and to the nation of inadequate education available to a large majority of our school population for another full generation?"[109]

To drive his point home, he quotes Julius Rosenwald (founder of Sears Roebuck) who in 1929 argued that our money has been given to us *in this moment* so we can provide the *fundamentals* to those who need them now, and whose loss will be irremediable if help comes to them later. Rosenwald had personal experience of help that arrived too late: "The millions that came to me at 50," he said, "could not restore a tooth I had lost at 30. They could not blot out a single day of grief."[110]

It's true that before we divert some of our money from wealth creation to philanthropy today, you and I have to take into account the heavy financial opportunity costs of such a diversion; but we dare not ignore the heavy personal opportunity costs paid by those whose lack of *fundamentals* today will leave them diminished for years—perhaps decades or even a lifetime.

The immediate plight of others is a strong reason to give at least some of our money now, and give it to organizations that will use our gift to address today's problems rather than to increase endowments that, years from now, may or may not help those who come after us.

Giving Now Keeps Money from Misuse by the Government

Giving money and power to government is like giving whiskey and car keys to teenage boys.*

P. J. O'Rourke (b. 1947)

There's no way I can tell who will be in office when you read this paragraph: it may be conservative Republicans, conservative Democrats, some variation of a liberal administration, or an administration whose policies are a hodgepodge cobbled together to get it elected.

Who's in power is really irrelevant to my argument that you ought, within the limits of what's reasonable and legal, to keep your wealth from being taxed into the hands of the government. Even if I agree with the ends an administration seeks to achieve, I still think that private individuals are likely to make better use of those same funds.

It's not just because I agree with the Italian proverb that says "Public money is like holy water; everyone helps himself to it." It's also because money that falls into the hands of the government is deprived of all three of the incentives that make private property such a useful tool.[111]

Recall that earlier, relying on St. Thomas Aquinas, we saw that there are three quite practical reasons that justify private property:

1. Because people tend to take better care of their own property than they do of community property, private ownership makes for better care of all property.

---

* P. J. O'Rourke, "Why God Is a Republican and Santa Claus Is a Democrat," preface to *Parliament of Whores* (1991). In "The Winners Go to Washington, D.C." in the same book, O'Rourke says: "For the people in government, rather than the people who pester it, Washington is an early-rising, hard-working city. It is a popular delusion that the government wastes vast amounts of money through inefficiency and sloth. Enormous effort and elaborate planning are required to waste this much money."

2. When some of the goods of the earth are clearly designated mine and others designated yours, and these divisions are publicly recognized by law, there tend to be fewer disputes within society.

3. If I know that I will own (and thereby be able to use and enjoy) the fruits of my labor without the undue interference of others, I'll likely work harder to draw from my property the good things it can yield.[112]

Taxation takes private wealth and makes it public. It renders that now-public property susceptible to each of the three deficiencies that the institution of private ownership remedied in the first place.

In that way, and no matter how virtuous and wise the presiding government might be, there's a great likelihood that the wealth taken by the government through taxation will be used less efficiently for the common good than it would have been had it remained in the hands of individuals, and it may even be used foolishly.*

Ronald Reagan in the mid-1960s noted some of the less responsible ways in which tax money wound up being spent:

> We are for aiding our allies by sharing some of our material blessings with those nations which share in our fundamental beliefs, but we are against doling out money government to government, creating bureaucracy, if not socialism, all over the world. We set out to help 19 countries. We are helping 107. We spent $146 billion. With that money, we bought a 2-million-dollar yacht for Haile Selassie. We bought dress suits for Greek undertakers, extra wives for Kenya government officials. We

---

* Although government involvement generally guarantees a decline in the efficiency with which wealth is being used, it would clearly be foolish to oppose all taxation. If the government did not undertake certain public projects or finance certain kinds of goods and services, they would not provided, and all would suffer. I don't say that all taxation is imprudent; just that we should generally try to minimize the amount of money that falls into the less-efficient hands of the government.

bought a thousand TV sets for a place where they have no electricity.[113]

Giving money to charity today keeps it from being taxed tomorrow, and thereby withholds at least that much money from the less efficient hands of the government.

Giving Now Enables Us to Fulfill the Obligations of Our Money

> *I have never had the opportunity of knowing, by experience, how [possession of money] makes one feel. It is something to have been spared the responsibility of taking charge of the Lord's silver and gold.*[114]

Lucy Larcom (1824–1893)

Apart from the government's inefficiency, there's a greater reason—you might even call it a metaphysical reason—for you to give some of it away today so that it doesn't fall into the hands of the government.

As I indicated earlier, it's no accident that you have the money and the talents you have. For reasons that neither you nor I can fathom, you and I have been born into the world in this era rather than a thousand years ago or a thousand years from now; we've been given the opportunities that, through ingenuity, effort, or luck (or all three), have brought us a considerable amount of *non-essential wealth*.

Now here I am standing on your doorstep telling you that none of this is a matter of chance: it's no accident that you and I have wealth greater than we need for our own *fundamentals*. It's been put into our hands for a specific purpose: you and I have been chosen as instruments to use our *non-essential wealth* to help bring about the universal destination of goods.

You and I.

Not the government.

Because you and I can use it more efficiently and with greater wisdom than can the government.

Best of all, you and I are not, like a hammer in the hands of a carpenter, brute instruments that serve passively, not knowing the end for which we're used; we're intelligent instruments. Indeed, we're simultaneously the carpenter and the tool the carpenter uses to bring about the universal destination of goods.

My money is a calling for me, and yours is a calling for you.

Relying on your intelligence and understanding and your money, you must, insofar as you can, shape your own life in accordance with the values you hold; and you must seek to use your talents and your money to help others benefit from those same values. In the same way that money derives its meaning from the ends it serves, so your life derives its meaning from the ends that you and your money serve.

◆ ◆ ◆

In the ant's house, the dew is a flood.

Here you stand in this moment in time with your talents and understanding and money. There, opposite you—sharing the earth you walk upon, breathing the air you breath, looking up to the same stars you see at night—there, opposite you, and in this same minute, stand countless souls lacking the *fundamentals*: hungry children who could be fed with a few dollars and educated with a few dollars more; grownups with chronic illnesses that could be cured with medicines cheaply available here but not where they live; laborers who, with a few months' training, could learn skills that would lift them, their families, and their nations out of desperation, making them partners with you in helping to realize the universal destination of goods where they live, even as you turn your attention elsewhere.

For that matter, there's the anger, bitterness, despair, and envy that plague our very neighbors—from the middle class to the wealthy—many of whom seem to have lost their way spiritually, and in ever increasing numbers their lives and families are being destabilized and torn apart.

These men and women are partners with you on this earth at this moment; and, directly or indirectly, you are called to be a means whereby they come to share in the goods of the earth—material and spiritual—that were put here for the well-being of all.

I don't claim that any of these specific tasks I've just listed are ones to which you have been called. I claim only that the meaning of your life and your money is partly a function of the way in which you use your life and your money to help realize the universal destination of goods.

As John D. Rockefeller noted,

> It is the duty of men of means to maintain the title to their
> property and to administer their funds until some man, or

body of men, shall rise up capable of administering for the general good the capital of the country better than they can.[115]

In a word, you are indispensable in accomplishing that part of the task that has been given to you. In all of creation and for all of time, no other person has received the singular combination of background, talents, and opportunities that are yours alone. No one can help bring about the universal destination of goods in just the way you can.

That you have such money, a unique background, and your own talents and opportunities is a sign that you have a particular calling, a task, a responsibility that is your own and not anyone else's. You should not lightly, by means of inactivity or taxes, yield to others or to the government those tasks that are yours alone to accomplish.

Giving Now Forms Us in Virtue

Be charitable before wealth makes thee covetous.[116]

Sir Thomas Browne (1605–1682)

There's a second, quite personal reason why we shouldn't devote all our *non-essential wealth* to the creation of more wealth, but should instead give some of it away now.

Earlier, we considered a number of grave dangers that threaten those of us who spend *non-essential wealth* on ourselves: it complicates our lives, breeds impatience, can aggravate bad personality traits, tempts us to engage in vanity spending, and even may lead us to try to use our money to bring about the pseudo-resolution of real human problems. None of those things are good for us as persons or good for those we love and who depend on us. No one is ever immune to these dangers in money, whether the wealth is great or not, non-essential or not, and whether it's idle or being used to create new wealth.

Rich or poor, we're all vulnerable to the attractions of the things of this world, and we're all capable of growing so attached to them that they overthrow us. That old woman was dragged into Hell by her wealth: one potato!

I grant that there never was such a woman; it's just a folk tale. But like many folk tales that have come down to us, it contains a genuine insight into the human condition: attitudes corrupt us, not things.

Because she valued that potato more than her life and her soul, that old woman was destroyed by it. Those of us who grip our *non-essential wealth* as if it were ours alone—and meant to serve us alone—exalt ourselves above material creation and even above other people who are truly needy. Like the old woman, we risk being dragged into Hell by our selfishness.

Not all of the poor are as covetous as the old woman grasping her potato. For many, poverty can even be a school of virtue. As St. Thomas Aquinas notes,

> The privation of one's possessions, or poverty, is a means of perfection, since by doing away with riches we remove certain obstacles to charity; and these are chiefly three. The first is the

"Shortly after I realized I had plenty, I realized there was plenty more."

cares which riches bring with them. . . . The second is the love of riches, which increases with the possession of wealth. . . . The third is vainglory or elation which results from riches.[117]

Now I'm not suggesting that you embrace poverty.

But to keep your attitude toward your possessions from becoming grasping, you need to loosen your grip on some of it on a regular basis, and to do so cheerfully. You don't have to believe in God to grasp the fundamental truth in the psalm: "Blessed is he that considereth the poor and needy: the Lord shall deliver him in the time of trouble."[118]

In such generosity, there is wisdom, goodness, and virtue—all of which only come when you actually loosen your grip on your wealth.

Which is why you've got to give some of it away.

◆ ◆ ◆

But to whom?

We can try to avoid the dangers inherent in *non-essential wealth* by giving it to others close to us, but when we do that, other people come to have *non-essential wealth* and simply inherit the problems we're trying to avoid by giving it away. Especially if they're young or inexperienced in handling wealth responsibly, *non-essential wealth* may stifle their initiative, impoverish their humility and gratitude, and even threaten their integrity and identity as persons.[119]

We can try to avoid the dangers inherent in *non-essential wealth* by using it all for wealth creation. Initially, that seems a better choice than giving it away because it keeps the money out of the hands of those who may use it less wisely than we will. Also, those of us who do employ our *non-essential wealth* for wealth creation find that the harsh demands of running a successful business reduce some of the moral risks inherent in wealth. As James Russell Lowell noted almost a hundred years ago, "There is no better ballast for keeping the mind steady on its keel, and saving it from all risk of crankiness, than business."[120] The Bible, which so often calls upon the rich to give away their wealth, praises the virtue of good businessmen: "Seest thou a man diligent in his business? He shall stand before kings; he shall not stand before mean men."[121]

Part of the reason is that success in business imposes on those of us at the top a kind of asceticism: long hours at work, single-mindedness, sustained intensity, and devotion to goals which may not be accomplished for months or even years. The best businessmen are disciplined and, in many ways, even austere. They know that self-indulgence impairs the efficiency of those who bear responsibility.

Unfortunately, when we choose austerity of life in order to be more efficient, we're not virtuous in the deepest sense of the word: we've chosen austerity as a means to an end beyond itself, not because we see that an austere life is good in itself. In such cases, our austerity is a tactic, not a moral virtue.

And of course, there are some vices (like pride, impatience, and imperiousness) that can even, for a long time at least, coexist with success at the top, especially when the person at the top is the one who has financed much or all of the business with his own *non-essential wealth*.* I won't seek here to catalog the vices that are consistent with (at least short-term) business success, for my purpose is more limited: I only mean to point out that

> *Even for those of us who have a vocation to create wealth,*
> *devoting all our non-essential wealth to wealth creation*
> *is not a sure defense against the moral and other risks inherent*
> *in non-essential wealth.*

---

* As Emerson notes in his essay "Wealth": "Next to humility, I have noticed that pride is a pretty good husband. A good pride is, as I reckon it, worth from five hundred to fifteen hundred a year. Pride is handsome, economical: pride eradicates so many vices, letting none subsist but itself, that it seems as if it were a great gain to exchange vanity for pride. Pride can go without domestics, without fine clothes, can live in a house with two rooms, can eat potato, purslain, beans, lyed corn, can work on the soil, can travel afoot, can talk with poor men, or sit silent well-contented in fine saloons."

Indeed, by seeking to fulfill the second vocation of the wealthy (wealth creation) we may fail to fulfill the first one (virtue). Former Australian Prime Minister Robert Menzies put it this way:

> A man may be a tough, concentrated, successful money-maker and never contribute to his country anything more than a horrible example. A manager may be tough and practical, squeezing out, while the going is good, the last ounce of profit and dividend, and may leave behind him an exhausted industry and a legacy of industrial hatred. A tough manager may never look outside his own factory walls or be conscious of his partnership in a wider world. I often wonder what strange cud such men sit chewing when their working days are over, and the accumulating riches of the mind have eluded them.[122]

It's imperative that we not let ourselves become that kind of wealth creator.

◆ ◆ ◆

In principle at least, I accept the conclusion that my *non-essential wealth* is meant to help bring about the universal destination of goods. But I confess that, unless I'm vigilant, like the old woman I sometimes find my hands involuntarily tightening around the things that are mine.

In the introduction I mentioned that my life is a work in progress. Over the past few years I've come to understand and am working hard to embrace the principles enunciated in these pages. But, as I also said in the introduction, I'm not there yet.

Two thousand years ago, Cicero warned us:

> Beware of an inordinate desire for wealth. Nothing is so revealing of narrowness and littleness of soul than love for money. Conversely, there is nothing more honorable or noble than indifference to money, if one doesn't have any; or than genuine altruism and well-doing if one does have it.[123]

"The poor are getting poorer, but the rich are getting richer. It all averages out in the long run."

I truly believe that Cicero is right.

Then again, it's easy to think we're virtuous when we're not.

For those of us who have the vocation to create wealth, it's easy to think we're working twelve-hour days to bring about the universal destination of goods when, in fact, we're just out there slugging it out, making money, heedless of the sufferings of those who lack the *fundamentals* today.

To keep me straight, to keep me mindful to the universal destination of goods and to keep my grip on my money looser than the old woman's grip on her potato, I regularly take one more step, and it's a step I believe you should take, too, no matter whether you have a vocation to create wealth or not.

Every year I make myself give away some of my money, even though I know I might be able to use that money to create more. I give to a number of public charities that serve the poor and needy directly. Some of my contributions go to politicians whom I believe share my understanding of how the government should promote the general welfare. Sometimes I provide assistance directly to individuals who need more than their circumstances enable them to earn.

Here I'm not so much concerned with the forms of giving you engage in; I mean only to say that those of us who have a vocation to create wealth ought regularly to hold back some of the wealth we could use for that purpose, and simply give it away.

In light of what I've said so far about a vocation to create wealth, giving money away now seems both counterintuitive and counterproductive, perhaps even foolish. If we could use that money to bring greater wealth to many more later, wouldn't it be better to hold on to it, to keep working it and investing it while we're sharp? That way, there will be more money for so long as we continue creating wealth, and more money to give away when we're ready to do that in later years.

The wealth we create today and tomorrow, we mean to give away on the third day.

But there's a big gap between "mean to" and "doing." By always

"Being in possession of great wealth made me a bit self-conscious at first, but I finally came to terms with it."

postponing until tomorrow the day on which I actually have to re-linquish full control of my money, I risk believing that I'm increasing my money for the good of others when in fact I'm just increasing my wealth.

Is virtue the real motive that I delay my giving?

It may be that I'm deceived, and that beneath the appearance of generosity there lies deep in my soul the attitude of the old woman, "It's mine! You can't have it!"[124]

◆ ◆ ◆

I know myself pretty well.

Why, then, would I suspect that deep within me lurks such a bad attitude?

Because sometimes, even in good moments when I'm about to send a charity a check, I encounter irrational doubt. What if the market declines or my new business fails? This is money I could use later to jumpstart another business, but if I spend it on a contribution now, I won't be able to act as quickly and as vigorously in my businesses as I may need to act later.

At that point, those questions can't be explained as due diligence; they're simply a new hurdle to my releasing my grip on some of my money. For that reason, although I abhor selfishness and repudiate it in principle, I have to ask whether my irrational hesitation to let go of that money by writing a check could be rooted in the same self-ishness that caused the old woman to hold onto her potato.

If that's the case, then, so long as I've previously exercised due dili-gence in evaluating the recipients of that contribution, forcing my-self to write that check is a moral counterweight to the selfishness that lurks in the souls of all of us, and would take us over if we let it.

◆ ◆ ◆

You may remember that in the first part of this book as we sought to determine how much money is enough, we used the president as an example of someone who has heavy *profession-related needs*. To do his job, he needs a huge house, a large staff, numerous limousines, planes, helicopters, many maids, chefs, and a dining room that seats 240 several evenings of the week!

I said that he knows that these perks are only his to use, not to have, and to use only for a few years. For a term or two, the president controls those assets—not, however, as owner of them, but only as a trustee. He knows he must use them to fulfill his vocation, and then, when his term ends, he must instantly and completely relinquish them.

That ought to be for him a school of detachment; and it's certainly a model for us who will be on this earth only for a time and will be forced to yield all of our assets at the end of our term here.

The funny thing is that the White House isn't usually a school of detachment.

The people who work there come to enjoy their perks; they grow attached to them, come to take them for granted. At the end of the term, they're often jarred by the fact that they have to give them up. Without realizing it, they've become like the old woman with her potato.

Unfortunately, none of us are exempt from this tendency to view the things around us as simply ours, rather than as goods over which we serve only as trustees, charged with the duty to use them to provide our own *fundamentals* and the *fundamentals* of others. We have to fight this natural tendency to claim as absolutely our own the things we have.

I pray that I won't succumb to this tendency, but I've also found that prayer is not sufficient; I've got to fight it daily. I've found that one of the best ways to do so is *regularly* to give some of my money away.

*Only actually and regularly giving away
some of our money fosters the spirit of detachment
we're all called to have toward the goods of the earth.*

"I'm not a machine, Deborah. I can't just turn my greed on and off."

Regularly giving keeps me mindful of the meaning and purpose of my money; it helps sustain in me the spiritual detachment toward my money that's essential if I hope to use it for others without resentment and to continue doing so cheerfully, day after day and year after year.

That's why I'm convinced that, for the sake of our souls, and particularly while we're actively engaged in creating wealth, we dare not refrain from giving generously—and doing so regularly.

◆ ◆ ◆

Now it may be that the resistance to giving that I sometimes experience is not rooted so much in the vice of selfishness as in the lack of four primary virtues I should have, virtues that would make giving easier and would make me a better person.

Faith in Providence

No matter how well I've evaluated a charity, I can't see the future or read souls. Giving money to others for them to use to help bring about the universal destination of goods is a chancy business. In many ways, it's a leap of faith that tests our confidence in other persons and in God's providence. We know that money can corrupt those who receive it, and can even corrupt organizations. Even those who are not corrupted by our contribution may grow lax because of it or waste the funds we supply to them.

Giving money away brings me up against my professed conviction that God will guide the hands of others in their work just as, I believe, He has guided mine. Writing a check forces me to act on that faith, and when—a few months or a year later—I see my gift misused, it forces me to trust that, in the grand scheme of things and so long as I acted prudently and in good faith, contributing was the right decision and, ultimately, good will come from my generosity even though I cannot at the moment see how.

Giving money away also tests my faith that, if things in my businesses go wrong or the economy fails, God will nonetheless provide us with that which we need. Like me, you probably often find it hard not to store up wealth for a rainy day, hard to give it to those who are suffering in the rain that's falling on them today.

Humility

Contributing some of our money to others also requires a measure of humility and forms us in humility. When I turn over some of my money to others for them to use as they see fit, I acknowledge that they may be able to do more good with that money in their field than I can in mine.

That's not an easy judgment for me to make, and it's probably not easy for you. Like most folks in business, I'm pretty confident. I've got successes to justify much of my confidence. It's frankly hard for me to acknowledge that others may be better at using my money than I am. And that makes it hard for me to give money away, even money that I know the recipients intend to use to help bring about the universal destination of goods.

In a word, whereas creating wealth for the good of all leaves you and me comfortably in charge, giving money away cedes control

*"If God hadn't wanted there to be poor people,
He would have made us rich people more generous."*

over that money to others and even, potentially at least, diminishes the control we have over our own lives and destiny. It tests our humility and actually calls us to develop greater humility and to rely more on providence, not in principle or imagination, but in fact.

Generosity

If we balk at giving money away today, how much harder will it be for us in the future to give away that greater amount of wealth we claim we're creating to use for others later? I think that those of us who are creating wealth now need regularly to practice giving now, so that later we'll have the strength of character and the virtue of generosity it will take to give away the greater amounts that our wealth creation will bring us.

Like typing, dancing, sewing, and so many other skills, giving is only learned by doing. The more we do it, the easier it becomes, and—often—the greater the desire grows to do more of it and do it more often. Generosity today awakens in us greater generosity tomorrow, and an attitude of public-spiritedness.

Good example

Now although serving as an example is not virtue in itself, it does promote virtue in others. Giving today (even when we could use that money to create more wealth) can inspire others to approach us to seek to know what motivates our generosity with money that could be used to create more wealth. We may be able to help them discover the meaning of their own money and show them the wisdom of giving generously now and later to help bring about the universal destination of goods.

Better yet, our generosity today may awaken generosity in those we love and for whose character we are responsible: our children and our spouse, and others close to us who are particularly at risk because of the dangers inherent in wealth. Our example may help keep them from succumbing to the vices that afflict so many who have *nonessential wealth.*

◆ ◆ ◆

In sum, sharing our money with others awakens in each of us humility, generosity, and confidence in God's providence, each of which is an essential element in the life of virtue to which, as I noted earlier, all men and women, rich and poor, are called. For that reason, I'm convinced that even when we have a vocation to create wealth and are still adept at doing so, we must regularly give some of that money away.

We saw earlier that the value of our money comes from the ends for which we use it. Not all those ends are exterior to us: indeed, we must use our money not only to help others, but also as a means by which we perfect ourselves.

Forming ourselves in virtue
is a worthy use of our wealth,
even if we can only acquire that virtue
by giving some of that wealth away.

chapter 12

the best ways to give

BOOKSTORES AND LIBRARIES HAVE ON THEIR SHELVES DOZENS OF BOOKS ABOUT WEALTH AND GIVING, RANGING FROM WELL-CONSIDERED MANUALS TO RATHER TECHNICAL ARGUMENTS THAT DEMONSTRATE MATHEMATICALLY THAT, WITHOUT JEOPARDIZING THOSE PERSONS AND VALUES WE MUST PROTECT, EACH OF US CAN GIVE FAR MORE THAN WE THINK WE CAN.

It's not my purpose to re-create the arguments or advice found in these helpful works. I hope in this book to achieve three basic things:

1. To show you that your money has a meaning that is intimately bound up with the meaning of your life: you have been called to help bring about the universal destination of goods.

2. To show you the two paths that, since you have read this far

into this book, are likely the ones you're meant to follow as you bring about the universal destination of goods: w*ealth creation* alongside some form of *giving now*.

3. To get you to take the first, difficult steps down the path to regular, sustained giving.

Tithe Regularly

Set apart a tithe of all the yield of your seed that is brought in yearly from the field.

Deuteronomy 14:22

Earlier I mentioned that in the rough-and-tumble world of business, it can be hard to maintain a generous spirit and civic-mindedness: competition tends to stifle these virtues in us. If we don't struggle to nurture generosity in our souls and that openheartedness that's the root of giving, we're likely never to find time for giving, and grow ever more hardened as time goes by.

For so long as I'm still successfully creating wealth, I'm probably going to devote most of my *non-essential wealth* to creating more wealth. How much then must I hold back so I can give it away? How much must I give away to ensure that I develop and nurture the virtue of generosity and the habits of giving called for earlier?

Especially in rapidly changing economic conditions, that's hard to answer.

One solution is to refuse to commit to a specific percentage or amount and instead play it by ear, giving as opportunities arise and finances dictate—more in years when there are no great opportunities to increase our wealth through business and investments, and less in years when the opportunities to increase our wealth are many and great.

Along with many other formulas and methods, I've tried that one (as have a number of my friends) and it just doesn't work. It's like dieting as the mood strikes us or exercising when we find the time,

*"Oh, I'm really sorry. I just placed three million with
some broker who called five minutes ago."*

instead of following a predetermined plan and schedule. Those who
diet and exercise according to a plan and schedule actually get fit;
those who don't never slim down.

The same is true with giving.

> *When we don't follow a plan and schedule for giving,
> we find that, at the end of the day, we just never manage
> to give enough away.*

There are always new and better reasons to hold back . . . at least
until next week. But next week never comes without bringing another good reason to postpone giving yet again.

That's why I've concluded that regardless of our circumstances
and opportunities, all of us (from the poorest soul with only a potato to people with the wealth of Bill Gates) should discipline ourselves to give some of our wealth away regularly, *according to a
predetermined plan.*

A simple weekly, monthly, or yearly schedule sweeps away a thousand excuses and postponements and develops in us the habits of charity and public-spiritedness that each of us needs.

◆ ◆ ◆

So how much should we give on a regular basis?

I recommend that we tithe.

Yes, tithe.

Give 10%—the percentage that's been the standard for souls in the Judeo-Christian tradition for thousands of years. It's simple, but it's also wise with a wisdom that's caused it to survive as an accepted standard for hundreds of generations in cultures across the globe, in all kinds of circumstances, urban and rural, rich and poor.

Tithing is as old as the hills,
but for those just setting out on the path of giving,
it's also as solid and reliable as the hills.

Here's the wisdom in tithing:

Giving 2% or 3% is so little that it's not likely to be felt in your life; you won't miss 2% or 3%, and it won't make any difference in your soul.

Twenty percent or 30% is so much that, in hard times, you'll be seriously tempted to abandon your giving program altogether.

And once you start adjusting percentages according to circumstances, you're just like the person who adjusts his diet and exercise times to circumstances. You won't ever get in shape, as a person or as a giver.

Ten percent is a wise number, a good beginning—and for many, 10% is the most that can regularly be given without serious hardship. Begin there and you'll soon experience the wisdom of tithing.

◆ ◆ ◆

But 10% of what? I'm convinced that, minimally,

Those of us who have non-essential wealth
should give away 10% of that year's after-tax increase
in our net worth.

Ten percent is enough for each of us to feel the pain of giving, so it really does require a serious act of the will, which is what forms in us the virtue of generosity; but 10% of the after-tax increase in our net worth is not so much that our wealth creation efforts will be crippled by the lack of that money.

It leaves completely intact the wealth we had at year's beginning; it leaves in our hands 90% of the increase in net worth that our efforts have brought about; and thereby it leaves in our hands not only almost all of the wealth that is our tool for increasing wealth but also leaves intact the motivation that, as we discovered earlier, is one of the justifications for private property in the first place.

Plus, in many cases, 10% of the increase in our net worth will go far toward providing the *fundamentals* to many souls whose lives today are seriously diminished by their lack of them. In other words, giving away 10% of the increase in our net worth each year helps us develop the habit of generosity while serving the common good, now and in the future.

But 10% does more: it joins us to a wise tradition many thousands of years old, a tradition by which souls in times far poorer than ours voluntarily brought as gifts to the Temple the first fruits of their harvests—the finest grapes, the sweetest honey, the choicest olives, the prize sheep, and the fatted calf.[126] Thereby they acknowledged that the goods of the Earth were given to them by God—given to all men and women by God—and did not belong simply and absolutely to those who happened to bring them forth from their patch of field or meadow.

In our non-agricultural, capitalist society, money has largely taken the place of the fruits of the earth, but, as we saw at the beginning of this inquiry, the principle holds: the wealth even of our capitalist world doesn't belong simply and absolutely to those of us who hap-

pen to have brought it forth from our businesses. It is for the benefit of all mankind.

By offering 10% of the increase in our net worth each year, we
serve others less fortunate than we are. In humility, we join ourselves
to the wise tradition of offering in thanksgiving the first fruits of our
labor. We acknowledge that no matter how hard we may have
worked to earn it, that increase in our net worth is a gift to us; and
we affirm that our self-worth is measured not by how much we have
been given, but by our stewardship of what we've been given.

◆ ◆ ◆

But suppose we've not increased our net worth by much, or our net
worth has even declined?

Minimally,

> *We should give away the greater of 10 percent of that year's*
> *after-tax increase in our net worth, or 10 percent of the value*
> *of what we consumed on living expenses in that same year,*
> *taking into account the carrying costs of any assets that are*
> *already paid for, like a house.*

Otherwise, wealthy people whose net worth had not increased (or
had even declined a bit) would be exempt from giving. That
wouldn't be good for them personally, nor would it help bring about
the universal destination of goods.

◆ ◆ ◆

Tithing in this way won't quickly deplete the resources of those who
are adept at creating more wealth, nor will it even strip much wealth
from those who don't have a vocation to create wealth. Indeed, for
some of us, it may not even significantly reduce the rate at which our
wealth increases: with our productive lives and our opportunities for
increasing wealth greater than ever before, our wealth may soar even
while we give away 10% of our increased net worth every year.

I know that.

And some who read these pages may challenge me, arguing that I'm too lenient on those who have wealth. To bring about the universal destination of goods, shouldn't the wealthy give far more? Shouldn't they live as do the poorest of the poor?

Already our discussion of the *fundamentals* and especially of *profession-related needs* has shown why for those engaged in wealth creation, living like the poorest of the poor is not generally the best thing to do.

But let me approach this challenge from another direction.

Suppose I wrote a book on dieting and exercise for overweight people arguing that they should give up desserts each day and begin a regular but modest exercise regime. Even though those changes would not cause overweight folks to lose a substantial portion of the weight they need to lose, exercise and giving up desserts would be difficult for many of them.

Difficult but doable.

And because such a beginning program is doable, my weight-loss book might convince many to undertake the program as a beginning. Once they've experienced the benefits of being more fit and weighing less, and have developed the initial habits necessary to lose weight, these beginning dieters will be better able to accept my arguments for eating even less and exercising harder in a more rigorous weight-loss regime that would have quickly defeated them if they had begun with it.

When it comes to diet and exercise, I know how weak we are. To help the greatest number of people slim down and get healthier, I'm willing to be patient with beginners and help them take small steps initially so that they'll be more inclined to take bigger ones later.

I think the same approach is right for those who come to accept the universal destination of goods and, in principle, want to help bring it about, but have never engaged in serious financial sacrifice. In other words, when it comes to giving,

*We have to begin modestly
and develop the habit of generosity
one step at a time.*

For souls who have never taken giving seriously, regular, systematic tithing is a beginning, and a strong and satisfying one.

◆ ◆ ◆

In my life, I've come slowly to grasp the meaning of my wealth, to realize that it's been placed in my hands so that I can serve the common good by means of it. The dawning of this understanding has led me slowly to undertake first one and then another charitable work; slowly, I've managed to increase the number and value of contributions I make.

Writing this book has made it clear to me that I must do more, and I hope it has helped clarify for you what you're called to do, and how you must do it.

Nonetheless, even as I near the end of the task of writing a book showing how and why we have to bring about the universal destination of goods, I remain—as a person and a giver—a work in progress, as I'm sure you're a work in progress, too.

I'm walking down this road one step at a time, and I think you should be allowed to walk down it one step at a time, too, giving a bit here and a bit there, finding your footing, and not being forced by me or anyone else to seriously engage in giving until you're convinced of its wisdom, are sure of your footing, know what kind of giving is best for you, and are ready to take the next step.

◆ ◆ ◆

Earlier I quoted Margaret Thatcher: "No one would remember the Good Samaritan if he'd only had good intentions. He had money as well."

Like the Good Samaritan, we've got money.

And like the Good Samaritan, we've got good intentions and mean to start helping others very soon.

But, as I said, there's a big gap between "mean to" and "doing."

We've got to begin now to use our *non-essential wealth* for others.

Like all the generations of men and women—rich and poor—that have come before us, you and I are called to live a life of virtue, and to do it in this instant, not tomorrow. For most of the generations that have come before us, tithing has proven itself to be a strong and sustainable first step toward the proper use of the wealth that has been allotted each of them.

Tithing is only a beginning, but it's an important beginning.

Contribute from Capital Now

> Johnson: "From you having practiced the law long, Sir, I presume you must be rich." Edwards: "No, Sir; I got a good deal of money; but I had a number of poor relations to whom I gave a great part of it." Johnson: "Sir, you have been rich in the most valuable sense of the word." Edwards: "But I shall not die rich." Johnson: "Nay, sure, Sir, it is better to live rich than to die rich."[127]
>
> Samuel Johnson (1709–1784)

Most of us who have money want to accumulate more money, and we may even be pretty good at doing it. Sure, we'll tithe because tithing counteracts our natural tendency to grasp tightly whatever we have; it helps us learn to live generously. Beyond that, however, our tendency is to hold on to our money; to contribute to charity from earnings and to hold on to equity, working it hard to create more wealth we plan to give away later.

There's a measure of wisdom in this strategy.

It allows us to retain control over the bulk of the money that's been allotted to us in this life as our own obligation. It likely will increase the amount we can use for philanthropy later.

The problem with this strategy is that, in too many ways, my life is limited and so is yours. An accident could kill either of us tomorrow, or a heart attack or stroke. If that happens, who gets the money you've been using to create more wealth for charity later?

First then, in conjunction with your financial advisors, you want to ensure that you minimize the portion of your estate that goes to the government. We've already seen that, even apart from its politics, government is not the best steward of wealth. Letting a significant part of our wealth surge back into the public domain frustrates the purpose for which it was given to us.

We were indispensable in creating that wealth; we are the persons who have been called to use it for the common good. By not doing so, we risk allowing a significant portion of our money to slip from our hands into the coffers of the government, ensuring that it will never be used for the designated ends that we were called to use it for.

So where should it go?

If we're not extremely careful, when we die it will wind up in the hands of our heirs, not all of whom may be as convinced as we are that it should be used to help bring about good.

Our years of selfless creation of wealth that we intend soon to donate to charity may bring the opposite result: at our death, we may not only provide the government an infusion of money; we may provide a vacation home and a boat for an obnoxious relative and pay for his expensive divorce when he leaves his wife behind.

Recently, there was a couple who made careful plans to avoid any such diversion of their money into less than optimal uses, public and private. Husband and wife were trustees of a foundation that would receive his wealth at his death. Since the wife was significantly younger than the husband, they expected her to guide the foundation after his death, and to replace him with a trustee who would help carry out their intentions.

When both husband and wife were killed in an accident, control of the foundation went to the third person on the board, the secretary, who soon took the foundation in directions fundamentally opposed to the intentions of the couple who established it. Today, the

"And the bulk of my estate—my Venezuelan oil holdings,
my Malayan rubber plantation, my supermarket chain, my steel mill,
and my New York City real estate—I bequeath to the meek."

foundation is tangled in lawsuits by those who are seeking to wrench it back to the purposes for which it was established, and it's not certain what the outcome will be.

> *Because non-essential wealth has been placed*
> *in our hands, we are responsible for ensuring*
> *that it is used now and after our death*
> *to bring about the universal destination of goods.*

Letting the government tax it away from us or from our heirs is inconsistent with the responsibility given to us in particular to use it. Allowing individuals to spend it lavishly on themselves is also inconsistent with our obligation, and even leaves us partly responsible for the harm that comes to them if they use our wealth irresponsibly.

How can we avoid having our money fall back into the hands of the government, or prevent it from being used for private indulgence? Careful planning will help with the former. But we can go wrong even when we carefully choose those persons to whom we bequeath our wealth or give authority over its use. Money has a way of changing folks, surprising us and even surprising them.

It's imprudent to bequeath our *non-essential wealth* automatically to our relatives or thoughtlessly to others. Some of them may squander it quickly. To be honest, I've struggled to figure out how to choose a successor to handle my money, and I'm not entirely satisfied with any of the formulas I've come up with.

Nonetheless, in my will I've got to fill in a name or set of names. So based on what I know of others, I'm using my best judgment to ensure that what's left of my wealth when I die gets into the hands of persons who share my values: once their *fundamentals* are provided, they'll use the rest of my wealth for the common good.

At least I hope so.

I say "hope" not because I distrust my heirs. I don't.

But no one understands my obligations quite the way I do, or feels their force the same way; and, as we discussed in an earlier chapter, time and circumstance and money can change people, especially large amounts of money.

Far better, it seems to me, than burdening my heirs with money beyond their needs, and far more consistent with the principles and obligations we've described in this book, is that, before I die, I use all my *non-essential wealth* for the common good so that none is left over.

Yes.

Give it away while I'm still alive.

I think that's the best thing for me to do with it, and it's the best thing for you, too.

And we'd better begin doing that before our intellectual powers and business acumen start to decline. For even if death doesn't stop us cold before we use the bulk of our wealth for the common good, old age, distraction, and incompetence may. Diminishing powers of attention and declining acuity may even erode our ability to work our equity, causing our wealth to diminish even as we attempt to increase it.[128]

Whatever else you do, always remember this: *the money has to go somewhere.*

Unless we burn it, it cannot *not* be spent.

Any money that we don't spend, somebody else will: the government, our heirs, someone else. You don't have to be religious to accept the truth of what St. Augustine noted seventeen hundred years ago:

> It is not earthly riches which make us or our sons happy; for they must either be lost by us in our lifetime, or be possessed when we're dead, by whom we know not, or perhaps by whom we would not.[129]

Since you and I have, by virtue of our money, incurred a considerable responsibility to serve the common good with it, and since you and I understand that responsibility and know that we have it, it's far better that we do the spending than that someone else do it when we're no longer able. Others can't fulfill for you and me the responsibility that has been given to us.

All of us, men and women, should heed the challenge that Harriot Hunt issued to the wives of the wealthy 150 years ago:

> Daughters of inherited wealth, or accumulated labor! The wide door of philanthropy is open peculiarly to you! Your life-work lies beyond your threshold: your wealth has placed you above the sorrowful struggle for daily bread which takes up the whole time of so many of your brothers and sisters. You are the almoners of God. A double accountability is yours.[130]

A double accountability is ours.

So, in conjunction with our family members and with the advice of our financial professionals, we've got to assess our financial situation to discover how much of our equity we can devote to the common good today without impairing our ability to provide the *funda-mentals* tomorrow for ourselves and those who depend on us.

Then, considering our age and the number of years we'll likely continue to live (and taking due care to ensure we can continue to provide the *fundamentals* for those for whom we are responsible), we should not merely tithe the greater of 10% of our living expenses or of the increase in our net worth. In calculating what we give each year, we should also take into account our age and net worth. Specifically,

> *We should undertake a lifetime distribution program*
> *that will enable us to give away most (if not all) of our*
> *non-essential wealth by the time we die.*

Only that way can we ensure that the *non-essential wealth* that has been placed in our hands to be used for the common good will in fact be used for that purpose. The obligation to serve the common good came with our *non-essential wealth*; we must not risk failing to fulfill that obligation by passing that money on to others who may not see the obligation as clearly as we do, or who may choose not to fulfill it.

Now if we knew the day on which we'll die, we could ensure that our *non-essential wealth* would be distributed prior to that day. Lacking that knowledge, the best we can do is make a good faith effort to calculate a lifetime rate of distribution today that should result in all our *non-essential wealth* being distributed before we die.

The simplest way is just to divide our *non-essential wealth* by the number of years the actuarial tables say we have left to live. The quotient is the minimum we should give to charitable endeavors this year, drawing down our net worth. (Since our life expectancy and *non-essential wealth* change each year, we need to make this lifetime distribution calculation anew each year, and adjust our giving accordingly.)

Depending on our financial circumstances, some years our

lifetime distribution formula will trigger larger contributions than will tithing; other years, tithing may yield greater donations.

Young people who are rapidly increasing their net worth are likely to give more by tithing; older men and women with the same earnings as rising young people but with greater accumulated wealth will give more by drawing down their net worth based on their lifetime distribution calculation.

Here, then, is the complete formula for giving that, I believe, enables us to live in accordance with the meaning of the *non-essential wealth* we've been permitted to have:

> *Each year, we should contribute*
> *to the common good whichever is greater:*
> *(1) 10% of the increase in our net worth,*
> *(2) 10% of the value of what we consumed*
> *on living expenses in that year; or*
> *(3) An amount equal to our net worth divided by*
> *the number of years we can reasonably*
> *be expected to live.*

There may be years in which we complete our calculations, know how much we should give, but in good faith may be tempted to give less—we may not be able to find satisfactory recipients for that year's contributions or we may not have the time to seek them out. In such cases, it's certainly permissible to postpone distributing that year's portion of our *non-essential wealth*, but I think it's risky: the temptation not to give is always strong, and yielding to it easily becomes a habit.

In cases where, for one reason or another, we can't find suitable recipients for this year's gifts, I think we ought nonetheless to find some way to give up ownership of it, to transfer it to a family foundation or equivalent legal entity, so that even if we may still be able to determine the ultimate disposition of that money, it will no longer be ours and we won't be able to spend it on ourselves. The discipline of living in accordance with our giving formula each

*"The pivotal issue, then, is not whether you respond
to my needs by cash or by check but for how much."*

year (even if only by transferring our contributions to an entity
such as a family foundation) will do us more good spiritually than
will holding on to the money until we find a charity that fulfills
our criteria.

The more we pursue this disciplined course of action, the closer
we will come to accomplishing (as we ought) three essential
objectives:

1. We keep as much of our *non-essential wealth* as possible out
   of the hands of those who would be inefficient in using that
   wealth and might even use it for ends we consider repre-
   hensible.
2. We ensure that more of our *non-essential wealth* serves the
   common good, instead of being diverted to private use by
   those who may come to control it after we're no longer able
   to control it ourselves.

3. We fulfill the particular responsibility for the right use of this wealth that was given to us and to no one else.

These are worthy ends, and the souls who accomplish them in this life show themselves to be good and faithful stewards of the wealth placed in their hands.

chapter 13

let *giving now* be a
school of virtue

*Nobody should be rich
but those who understand it.*[131]
—Johann Wolfgang von Goethe
(1749–1832)

ONCE YOU DECIDE TO DEVOTE MORE OF YOUR *NON-ESSENTIAL WEALTH* TO THE COMMON GOOD, YOU'VE GOT TO DETERMINE WHO SHOULD HELP YOU CHOOSE THE RECIPIENTS OF YOUR CONTRIBUTIONS AND THE MEANS BY WHICH YOU WILL TRANSFER MONEY TO THOSE RECIPIENTS. THESE DECISIONS WILL AFFECT NOT ONLY THE CHARITIES THEMSELVES, BUT CAN HAVE A PROFOUND EFFECT ON YOU PERSONALLY, AND ON THOSE YOU LOVE—A GOOD EFFECT OR A BAD EFFECT, ACCORDING TO HOW YOU PROCEED.

As I noted earlier, there are already dozens of books out there that discuss the merits of the many vehicles for giving.[132] Making the right choice is important but beyond the scope of this book, so I won't attempt to sketch all the possibilities. To discover what's best for you, you need to discuss your options with your lawyers and accountants. Then you should go over those possibilities with close family members and others you trust or will involve in these decisions. For although you and I may now be convinced that it's right for us to give away some of our *non-essential wealth*, others who are close to us may not.

*Especially if our earnings are great, even our decision
to tithe may be experienced as a threat to the present or future
well-being of those who share our wealth now
or expect to inherit it when we die.*

As we grow in seriousness about our giving, we may sometimes feel that we have to break the grip that others thought they had on our money, even though, so long as we live, they have no legal claim on it. Whatever you do, proceed carefully: some ways of giving bring families together; some ways have little effect; and some break families apart.

In all your discussions and decisions about how much to give and where, keep in mind that as we seek to employ our *non-essential wealth* to serve the common good, we must do it in a way that draws us closer together and enriches, morally and spiritually, those we love and for whom we are most directly responsible. These people include our spouse, our children, and close relatives or others who may be affected by our decisions about our money.

I won't attempt here to second-guess your financial advisors or to substitute my judgment for yours about what's best for you and your family. I can, however, sketch the simple four-step program I'm using to minimize the stress of giving and to diminish the risks that my own *non-essential wealth* poses to my loved ones and me.

Indeed, I've found that this program has largely transformed my *non-essential wealth* from a threat into an instrument of virtue for me and for those I love. And it's doing this while serving the common good.

◆ ◆ ◆

The program's first two steps are interior, and it's likely—since you've gotten this far in this book—that you've already joined me in taking them (or are seriously considering doing so):

1. Understand and acknowledge the universal destination of goods.
2. From this point forward, strive to use your *non-essential wealth* to help serve the common good—by wealth creation insofar as that is appropriate, and by whatever other means are called for by your individual circumstances, talents, and responsibilities.

The third and fourth steps are exterior:

3. By precept, example, and participation, help others (and especially those you love) to come to share your understanding of the right use of *non-essential wealth*; and finally,
4. Create for them safe circumstances in which they can learn how to use *non-essential wealth* for those purposes, and by using it that way, develop in themselves the virtue of generosity and the habit of giving.

This last point is very important, since these individuals may later come to have control over that *non-essential wealth* which is yours to control today. For those of us who have wealth, the best way for our family members to learn about money is for them to handle it themselves in what I call a "school of philanthropy and virtue," a controlled environment in which they can distribute the money, but can't use it to harm themselves.

There are many ways to create such a school of philanthropy and virtue. Foremost is by example. If you want to teach others generosity, you've got to be generous yourself. When you give, you must give with good cheer—not resenting your obligation to use for the good of others what is yours, but remembering always to be grateful that God has given you the privilege of serving others in this manner.

If you fail to nurture in yourself the virtue of generosity or fail to exercise it regularly, all your other efforts to teach others generosity will have little effect.

Remember as well that since most family members—children especially—are not regularly involved in money decisions, then, if you want to teach your children not only a spirit of generosity but also how best to be generous with wealth, you also need to establish a regular means of involving them in your philanthropy.

So long as you regularly draw those close to you into your deliberations, it really doesn't matter whether you make your family's contributions directly to charities or indirectly by means of a family foundation, a donor-advised trust, or some other legal entity.[133] Yet let me emphasize that these deliberations need to be regular, not just now and then. Regular discussions about giving—and, even more importantly, regular contributions—show those close to us that, like exercising and dieting, stewardship must not be an afterthought or a matter of impulse, opportunity, or mood; it should be a planned, integral part of each of our lives.

◆ ◆ ◆

Goethe claimed that "nobody should be rich but those who understand it."[134]

When you make your family members partners in giving, they come to understand wealth and its obligations by their service as partners with you in giving. As appropriate, include among those who decide where you contribute parents, children, grandparents, and others, and even bring to meetings family members who are too young to serve as decision makers. There they'll see their elders working to use *non-essential wealth* to help bring about the universal destination of goods.

That example of generosity and serious public-spiritedness can have a profound impact on the worldview of the young persons in your family. As they grow older and are drawn more into deliberations and, finally perhaps, even given authority over some portion of your *non-essential wealth*, they will, in a controlled environment, come to experience the responsibilities and joys of effectively managing money for the good of others, while being shielded from the temptations that accompany money when it's simply ours to do with as we please.

Regular consideration of the various needs that are brought before our families affords opportunities for us to discuss with our spouse, our children, and other close family members the meaning of money itself and of our own money in particular, the values that inform our decisions, and even the unique personal vocation to which we find ourselves called. Such discussions are an excellent way to bring members of our families closer as, together, we come to know, understand, and share with each other some of the deepest values that human beings can embrace, the ones that are the foundation of all enduring communities: self-sacrifice, service, and love.

A family of persons aspiring to those values (and working to realize them in the family and in the world) will be strong, and its members less likely to succumb to the temptations inherent in *non-essential wealth*.

From the discussions in these meetings, families can come to know and learn to evaluate the many factors that need to be taken into account by those of us who aspire to be good stewards of our money. Those deliberations will help those we love learn to think selflessly about projects as they consider not the good that will come to them from the money expended, but the good that can be done for others with it. They'll learn to measure things by their worth, not by their price.

By weighing the requests that flood those who have money and by seeking out other causes the family might serve, those who are involved in the discussions will come into more contact with a wider variety of ideas and circumstances. This experience can remedy the problems that arise when our money, without our intending it,

*""And the Haves, you might say, are divided into the
Gives and the Give Nots."*

isolates us from persons less fortunate, leading us to forget just how
needy the world is.

I mentioned earlier that, not knowing the reasons for their
wealth, young people born into money can be afflicted with embar-
rassment about it and even guilt. Participating in discussions
wherein we choose to assist those who lack the *fundamentals* eliminates that irrational guilt, replacing it with the legitimate self-esteem
felt by those who, themselves having more than they need, use their
resources to help others who lack the *fundamentals.* They develop
the self-confidence that comes from doing good.

Indeed, those who direct their energy to the wise distribution of
wealth, instead of to the selfish consumption of it, become (and
come to see themselves as) what they should be: stewards using their
money to serve the common good.

Speaking of family values, essayist Barbara Ehrenreich noted that "At best the family teaches the finest things human beings can learn from one another—generosity and love. But it is also, all too often, where we learn nasty things like hate, rage and shame."[135]

Early involvement in philanthropic decisions is one way to try to keep the latter from happening, because it awakens greater generosity in us and can awaken greater generosity in our children.

In many ways, then, involvement of family in these serious deliberations wins for each of them a greater and earlier maturity than is often found in those whose *fundamentals* are already provided for, and who too easily get caught up in the frivolous affairs that lead some of the wealthy into trouble and sorrows, and give too many others a bad name.

Does drawing our family members into philanthropy with us guarantee that none of them will fall prey to the temptations inherent in *non-essential wealth*?

Certainly not.

We're all free creatures, and there's absolutely nothing we can do to guarantee that all of those we love will remain steadfast in virtue.

That's not news, but it's also not a phenomenon unique to the wealthy, and it's not a reason to refrain from doing those things that generally help form others (and even ourselves) in virtue.

Helping to decide how to use the family money to serve the common good forms the characters of those who serve. As our family members come to experience the power of private philanthropy to help valuable enterprises flourish, as they look into the faces of persons who have been helped or even saved by our family's generosity, they're likely to come to appreciate the importance and the joy of such giving, and to find themselves growing in the habits of generosity and civic-mindedness that characterize some of the very best human beings.

For those who have money, giving is an excellent way to neutralize the particular temptations that afflict us and those who are close to us, and to nurture virtue in ourselves and those we love.

Giving builds character.

Giving is a school of virtue for those who undertake it.

By having our family members assist us as we give today, we help them become better persons tomorrow.

This is a wonderful gift we can give to those we love.

chapter 14

begin today!

*It's easier for a camel to pass through the eye of a needle
than for a rich man to get into heaven.*
Matthew 19:21–25

THESE WORDS OF JESUS CHILL THOSE WHO HAVE MONEY AND ARE
CHRISTIANS, AND THEY JAR EVEN UPRIGHT NON-BELIEVERS, FOR
EACH OF US HAS EXPERIENCED IN OUR MONEY THE CORRUPTING
FORCE THAT PROVOKES CHRIST'S JUDGMENT.

How much money does it take for us to be among the rich about
whom Christ is speaking?

In Chapter 3 we sketched out ways to determine how much each
one of us needs for ourselves: the *fundamentals*. What's left over is
what makes us rich: *non-essential wealth*. And the more we have, the
richer we are.

We've cataloged the many ways in which *non-essential wealth*
threatens those who hold on to it. If we seek to avoid harm by giving it to others so that they wind up with *non-essential wealth*, then

they face the risks we just rid ourselves of. Spending it imprudently on ourselves was also no solution.

Should we burn it?

The universal destination of goods and the nature of property forbid that: wealth is not meant for us alone; it's not ours to burn. Rather we're only instruments by which the goods of the earth are meant to be made available to those for whom they are destined.

Avoiding the dangers of our *non-essential wealth* by destroying it betrays our primary responsibility to channel that wealth to those who lack the *fundamentals*.

It seems as if we're stuck with our *non-essential wealth*, yet still the words haunt us: "It's easier for a camel to pass through the eye of a needle than for a rich man to get into heaven." No wonder that, elsewhere in Scripture, it says, "The sleep of a laboring man is sweet, whether he eat little or much; but the abundance of the rich will not suffer him to sleep."[136]

◆ ◆ ◆

What, then, is to be done with our *non-essential wealth*?

It must become for us and for others a school of virtue even as we use it to provide the *fundamentals* to those who lack them.

Specifically, if we have a vocation to create wealth, we should devote it to the creation of new wealth that we can then, directly or indirectly, channel to those who lack the *fundamentals*. And, whether or not we have such a vocation, we should begin now to use some of our *non-essential wealth* for the present needs of others.

Because you and I are the ones who hold our money, you and I are the ones responsible for taking these steps to ensure that our *non-essential wealth* is used in accordance with the universal destination of goods. You and I are indispensable in this effort, and, the greater our *non-essential wealth*, the longer we must sustain our effort to ensure that it's used as it should be, and the more deeply involved we must be in that effort.

"It's easier for a camel to pass through the eye of a needle than for a rich man to get into heaven."

Yes, easier.

But not impossible.

When most of us read that Bible passage, we think of trying to thread a camel through a sewing needle. A thousand-year-old tradition understands the passage differently. It claims that in Jesus' time the Eye of the Needle was the name for one of the many gates in the wall that surrounded Jerusalem, a gate that was not very high at all. In fact, a standing camel couldn't get through the gate.

It was, however, possible for a camel to get through the gate—on its knees.

Therein lies the hope offered to you and me, and to every person who has ample *non-essential wealth*. As long as we walk proudly preening ourselves because of our money and success, we will not be able to enter heaven. But if we come to understand what our money—and our life—means, and humbly take up the task of living in accordance with that meaning, then, on our knees, even the wealthiest among us will be able to pass through the Eye of the Needle and enter heaven.

◆ ◆ ◆

I quoted Scott Fitzgerald's remark, "Let me tell you about the very rich. They are different from you and me." I also quoted Ernest Hemingway's cynical response, "Yes, they have more money."

You and I can change that.

Having come to understand the nature of property and the call to each of us that's embedded in it, you and I can employ our *non-essential wealth* to help serve the common good. We can be different, not because of our breeding or our selfishness, but because of our lives of service.

More than a hundred years ago, Andrew Carnegie wrote a brief essay called "The Gospel of Wealth" in which he sought to help others answer the call of wealth that he heard then. In these pages, I've tried to help you hear that call, too.

In our money and in our talent for creating wealth, we have discovered great goodness and hope, both for others and for ourselves. As we serve others by means of our wealth creation, our tithing, and our lifetime distribution of assets, we employ not merely our money but enlist even our souls in the service of our fellow men. We live in accordance with the gospel of wealth that Carnegie discovered in Christ's words. And in so doing, we have reason to hope that, when finally we pass from this life—tomorrow, the next day, or the day after that—we may be worthy of the promise given to those who, in this lifetime, have the privilege of being stewards of great wealth and the wisdom to exercise that stewardship well. Let Carnegie's concluding words in his "Gospel of Wealth" be mine, too, and yours:

> The gospel of wealth but echoes Christ's words. It calls upon the millionaire to sell all that he hath and give it in the highest and best form to the poor by administering his estate himself for the good of his fellows, before he is called upon to lie down and rest upon the bosom of Mother Earth.
>
> So doing he will approach his end no longer the ignoble hoarder of useless millions; poor, very poor indeed, in money, but rich, very rich, twenty times a millionaire still, in the affection, gratitude, and admiration of his fellow men, and—sweeter far—soothed and sustained by the still, small voice within, which, whispering, tells him that, because he has lived, perhaps one small part of the great world has been bettered just a little. This much is sure: against such riches as these no bar will be found at the gates of Paradise.

the next step

tips for wise and effective giving

*Nothing is impossible to the man
who doesn't have to do it.*
—Weller's Law

Okay.

You've committed yourself to tithing and you may even have begun the lifetime distribution of your assets.

Congratulations!

Now comes the hard part.

You'll soon find that though you may not be a billionaire, you've got fundamentally the same problem President Eisenhower's secretary of the treasury faced back in the fifties: "It's a terribly hard job to spend a billion dollars and get your money's worth."[137]

Even if you're just tithing, it's still hard to get your money's worth. For many people, 10% is a considerable amount of money, and we ought not to be writing checks for that kind of money without due diligence, especially since we're giving the money to promote the common good and don't want to give it to organizations that will use it inefficiently or for ends not consistent with our values.

Many a prudent contributor has at one time or another felt betrayed by organizations he thought he'd chosen well. It turned out that the charity he thought shared his values differed from him on substantive matters. I know of wealthy businessmen who made substantial contributions to universities, only to discover later that large percentages of the faculties of those schools spent time teaching their students to scorn the legitimate principles of business that make possible those large contributions.

> *Before you give, you need to know well the organization*
> *to which you're giving; and the larger your contribution,*
> *the better you need to know the entity that is receiving it.*

Even organizations that are fine when a donor chooses them can evolve into entities that promote values the opposite of those espoused by the donor. A friend of mine had dinner with a man who, in the 1950s, gave $500,000 to a major American university to create a chair of Catholic studies intended to promote a better understanding of Catholicism and a greater appreciation for it. At dinner with my friend some thirty years after making that contribution, that then-elderly donor almost wept when he admitted that the Chair of Catholic Studies he had endowed was now held by a professor whose claim to fame was his attacks on Catholicism. "That was the worst contribution I ever made," the old man said, looking down at his plate and shaking his head slowly from side to side.

The truth is that ultimately there's nothing we can do to *guarantee* that this won't ever happen to us. The risks we take in giving are not essentially different from the risks we take when, in marrying, we give ourselves to another. In each case, no matter how well we know the other, we're dealing with free creatures: human beings whose values may change over time, creatures who, for reasons of their own, may choose to violate even solemn commitments they've made to us.

From good marriages come great and important goods: the love of family members for each other, the formation of children in virtue and the raising of them up to lives of love and service. And from marriages gone wrong come lifelong enmity and children bitter and filled with dismay and hatred.

So, too, the "marriages" of donors and causes.

When donors become partners with a charity in doing good, that marriage provides the lost, the lonely, and the desperate the *fundamentals* they need to flourish as human beings; when donors choose without due deliberation, the marriage of donor and cause can squander wealth, set brother against brother, and yield a harvest of bitterness.

Risk is inherent in marriage and in every one of our dealings with other human beings. We can avoid it by never getting involved with others, by keeping a tight rein on ourselves, and by never committing ourselves or our wealth to other persons or entities.

That minimizes the likelihood we'll be betrayed, but it also ensures we'll never experience the joy of loving or being loved and the consolation of serving or being served.

Society and its manifold fruits—material, social, and spiritual—depend on our willingness to engage other human beings despite the risks inherent therein.

The universal destination of goods forbids us to hold back our selves or our fortunes; it calls us to serve one another according to our talents and circumstances, despite our knowledge that we may make mistakes or be betrayed.

As we saw earlier, by its very nature money signifies and brings about ever closer involvement of persons one with another, an involvement that lessens our independence and increases the risks to which we are exposed.[138] Interdependence increases benefits along with risks, and the greater our wealth, the more dependent we are on others for our enjoyment of it.

Seeing the critical importance of society to the well-being of each of us, a wise man doesn't refuse risks, he minimizes them. He seeks to ensure that, before he makes an irrevocable commitment of funds, he knows the recipients well.

An old Dutch proverb says that "The generous man enriches himself by giving; the miser hoards himself poor." We mustn't let wariness cause us to hoard ourselves poor; we mustn't hesitate to give because we may be betrayed.

Indeed, too severe a scrutiny of those to whom we give (or may give) can nurture in the soul such a distrust of others that the very love which originally motivated our charity gets snuffed out, and in the act of giving we become uncharitable: "And though I bestow all my goods to feed the poor, and though I give my body to be burned, and have not charity, it profiteth me nothing."[139]

In our giving, we must be prudent, but never hard.

ten rules of thumb
for donors

Having said that, it still remains true that fruitful giving must be built on prudence.

For that reason, over the years I've jotted down "Ten Rules of Thumb" that I use to guide my contributions, along with a couple dozen questions that make it easier for me, in any decisions, to see how those Rules apply to particular organizations that approach me or to causes that catch my eye.

The Ten Rules of Thumb aren't comprehensive—or perfect. I'm sure that each has exceptions, and not all of the questions are appropriate for all kinds of organizations. Nor are they completely consistent. You'll see that to abide by one, you may sometimes have to rely on another loosely or not at all. That's okay. They're here not to be an iron hand but as tools to help you judge where to give. Just as a carpenter selects the best tool for the job at hand, so you should select the Rules that best apply to the charity you're considering, and not be troubled if they all don't work equally well in helping you make your decision.

Even when used loosely this way, the Ten Rules of Thumb and the questions help me as I consider the many appeals I receive. Especially if you're new to giving, they may help you minimize mistakes and disappointments as you come to understand more deeply what your wealth means, and as you take up the serious task of living in accordance with its meaning. Let's consider the Ten Rules of Thumb one by one, and at the end of this discussion I'll list the supplemental questions that you should consider using. Here, then, the Rules of Thumb:

Rule of Thumb 1: The Principle of Indispensability
Support Indispensable Causes
to Which Your Support Is Indispensable

There are tens of thousands of nonprofits clamoring for help. Many of them address problems that seem less urgent to me than they do to their advocates. It may be that my own background, talents, and circumstances leave me deaf to their importance. Then again, it may be that I'm called to take up other tasks that, for that very reason, I understand well and seem urgent to me.

In discussions with those who know you well and perhaps even by trial and error, you'll slowly have to determine which role you're called to play in serving the common good, and whether it involves education, the hungry, the homeless, the arts, religion, or one or more of the countless other tasks that cannot be accomplished without the assistance of those of us who have extra wealth.

I've found that this first rule of thumb, which I call the *Principle of Indispensability,* helps me choose those causes best suited for me to support. My choice is rooted in a prior conviction: each of us is here on earth for a special reason. We're each expected to accomplish certain tasks and play particular roles. No one can take our place. Because in these respects we're indispensable, the world is diminished when we fail to discover those tasks that are ours alone—and when we're kept from accomplishing them.

My *Principle of Indispensability* is rooted in this conviction, and actually has two facets. First, I believe that *donors should be indispensable to the organizations they support.* The $100 a year I could give to a charity with a budget of hundreds of millions wouldn't make a significant difference to that organization, nor would $5,000 a year make even a marginal difference. To that charity, my financial assistance is not indispensable.

Now there may be organizations whose efforts I applaud and that I could help not only with a contribution but also with my knowledge, time, and efforts. However, if someone is already doing well what I could do, or if the organization has the funds to hire someone to do what I could do, it doesn't make sense for me to duplicate the effort of the person already there or take work from a person who could be hired.

My help is not indispensable, and I can do more good by going elsewhere and helping efforts that cannot succeed without my assistance. In this way, initiatives that can succeed without me do, and the ones that I support also succeed.

Second, I believe that the *charities to which we give significant help should themselves be indispensable.* In other words, their success should bring to mankind physical, intellectual, moral, or spiritual benefits of the most important kind, benefits without which mankind (or specific individuals) would be fundamentally diminished.

Now there are many foolish endeavors to which you and I might become indispensable in the first sense. Were we to support them, they might thrive; were we to turn away, they likely would die. Although we're indispensable to their existence, they themselves are not indispensable or even seriously important to mankind. I shy away from helping such groups, preferring instead to rely on the *Principle of Indispensability.*

> *Support indispensable causes to which*
> *our help is indispensable.*

Supporting indispensable causes to which our help is indispensable overcomes one of the most frustrating problems in assisting charities: the measurement of results.

In profit-making businesses, you and I measure our effectiveness by a single common measurement. No matter what product or service we provide, we can assess our investment by measuring dollars returned against the dollars invested. In philanthropy, there are no such common measures: one organization may feed 3,000 homeless each day, another may teach 500 inner-city children each year, and a third may publish classic books of wisdom.

Where is the common denominator by which to judge the importance of one against the other?

In my second example, where is the measure by which to determine whether the education is truly effective, and whether it is being done by this organization with greater efficiency than another organization engaged in a similar work? And how can we measure whether the education of these children actually does have a fundamentally transformative effect on them?

The lack of universal and easily ascertainable measurements makes dealing with nonprofits inherently frustrating. To overcome this problem, nonprofits have understandably fallen into the habit of advertising things such as the percentage of contributed income they spend on the work they were established to accomplish, the number of hours volunteers have contributed to that work, and other such gauges to indicate the scope of their efforts.

The problem here is that these numbers quantify *input*, not *results*.

They measure *effort*, not *effect*.

Were a business to adopt such standards, it wouldn't know which efforts were successful and which were losing most of the money expended on them.

In cases where legitimate objective measurements of results are hard to establish and employ, I fall back on the *Principle of Indispensability*. It would be wrong for me to refrain from helping an organization simply because it's engaged in indispensable work wherein it's intrinsically impossible to provide numerical measures of effectiveness (such as the work of parents). If the work itself is indispensable and my help is also indispensable, then it seems legitimate for me to support the endeavor.

Rule of Thumb 2: The Principle of Synergy
Seek Synergy

Generally speaking, we're more effective in business efforts to which we contribute not just money, but also knowledge, ability, time, and effort. And that's generally where we achieve our greatest returns. The synergy of knowledge, money, and energy usually provides a greater return than passive investments of money.

The same holds true in giving. The dollars you contribute can have a greater impact if, when you consider where to give your financial assistance, you rely on the *Principle of Synergy* which recommends that you:

> *Support initiatives that can benefit from the synergy*
> *of your knowledge, interests, wealth, and expertise.*

In practical terms, this means that you and I should contribute money to philanthropic activities in fields in which we're already actively and even eagerly involved. It's in these endeavors that our judgments of the charities tend to be keener, and our own contributions—financial and otherwise—are likely to prove indispensable.

In proposing this, I don't rule out all passive giving. There may be certain projects that, for other reasons, you should support, even if they can't benefit from the synergy of your knowledge, wealth, and energy. Nonetheless, the *Principle of Synergy* suggests that it's often more effective to support initiatives where there's great synergy.

Rule of Thumb 3: The Principle of Leadership
Know Who's in Control

In an ideal business, the owners/investors have complete control of their investments. They hire the right people to accomplish the objectives of the business and delegate to those people the responsibility and authority to do so.

In an ideal nonprofit world, donors would likewise have complete control of the use of their contributions. They would find the right people to accomplish the objectives of the charity and delegate to those people the responsibility and authority to do so.

Unfortunately, what's difficult in the business world is even harder in the nonprofit realm. Although many people establish their own businesses in accordance with their own notion of what will be profitable and how best it can be done, few set up charities. Generally we don't establish the charities that we wind up supporting; we're invited to support organizations or initiatives that are the product of someone else's vision and have been formed according to someone else's notion of the best way to implement that vision. Indeed, they may even have calcified into a form that will never meet even the basic standards of accountability by which we measure the profit-making enterprises in which we invest.

Many a time, persons soliciting help from me have either not understood my questions about their nonprofit organization's finances and internal controls, or have even seemed to find my questions inappropriate. After all, they're doing good work! What more can I ask? They want me to make a major contribution, but they also want me to trust that the goodwill of those running the charity will ensure that my money is spent wisely.

That's not sufficient in business, and it's often not sufficient in charities.

Where vigilance, tight controls, and objectively verifiable measures can be employed in charities, they should be, as long as they don't significantly degrade the overall work of the organization. Unfortunately, many charities are engaged in work where such measures are not widely possible. In those cases, responsibility for the efficiency and integrity of the institution depends heavily on the energy, intelligence, character, and integrity of those in charge.

For my part, when charities understandably can't provide independently verifiable evidence of their efficiency and effectiveness, I do my best by relying on my *Principle of Leadership:*

Know the leaders of the organization,
and keep an eye on the organization
by staying close to its leaders.

You'll find that this is easiest in local organizations, and that's reason enough to keep your charity local, if you can.

That, however, brings with it another consideration, particularly if you wind up making large contributions to a local organization. No matter how many others contribute to it and no matter how little day-to-day involvement you have with the organization, you're likely to be presumed to be a controlling party. That means that, like it or not, you'll be held responsible when anything goes wrong: the greater your financial responsibility for an organization, the more your reputation will be linked to it, for good or for ill. That's all the more reason to rely on the *Principle of Leadership*—know who's in control and stick close to them.

Rule of Thumb 4: The Principle of Anonymity
Consider the Pros and Cons of Anonymity

Whereas humility calls us to do good works anonymously, public giving fuels giving by others. News that one person has given generously spurs others to contribute generously, too. Often we can serve a cause simply by letting it be known that we've contributed to it.

Unfortunately, intrinsic to money and its privileges is the temptation to pride—a pride rooted in the understandable but erroneous notion that because we have money, we somehow deserve it and are better than others who lack money. Large contributions made publicly increase the temptation to pride and self-satisfaction by bringing us praise and the attention of many who otherwise would remain indifferent to us.

Then there's the danger that we just mentioned: if others know that we've donated large amounts to an organization, our own reputation can be sullied by the misdeeds of that entity.

Better to give anonymously, we could conclude—except that

anonymous giving has its own temptations, exposing us to a smug-
ness that may be even more insidious than the pride that comes from
being acclaimed. It becomes easy to look down on others who think
they know us, but have no real idea of the secret life we live as
donors, giving thousands here and thousands more there.

Since there are risks in both public giving and in giving anonymously, it seems to me the best approach is simply to forget ourselves, and, except for the call to service inherent in it, to push out
of our minds what we think our wealth and our giving says about us
personally. Push any concern with ourselves out of our minds and
ask one simple question: "In this particular case, what is best for the
cause that I seek to support with my contribution?"

In general, I think anonymity is to be preferred, but there will be
times when associating our giving with a project will help it consid-
erably. In such cases, insistence on anonymity is an indulgence, not
to be admired. Hence, my *Principle of Anonymity:*

> *Consider the pros and cons of anonymity,*
> *and choose that which serves best*
> *the cause you are supporting.*

Rule of Thumb 5: The Principle of Dependency
Do Not Foster Dependency

Andrew Carnegie maintained that those "who have wealth give
millions every year which produce more evil than good, and really re-
tard the progress of the people, because most of the forms in vogue
today for benefiting mankind only tend to spread among the poor a
spirit of dependence upon alms, when what is essential for progress is
that they should be inspired to depend upon their own exertions."[140]

Carnegie's judgment echoes those of the rabbis of the Talmud
who taught that the primary purpose of charity is to help others help
themselves. Also, many Talmudic laws sought to protect the poor
from the shame of dependency, emphasizing the dignity of the charity recipient. The Talmud notes that when Rabbi Yannai saw some-

one giving alms to a poor man in public, he rebuked him: "It would have been better not to give him anything at all, rather than give it in such a way that you put the poor man to shame."[141]

Shielding the deserving poor from the shame of dependency is excellent. Even better is assistance that helps free the poor from dependency. This is why, as you consider charities to support, you should investigate those that don't foster dependence, but help the dependent become independent—including the charities themselves.

Consider as well what the rabbis of the Talmud deemed the most meritorious form of dispensing charity: loans, which recipients are expected to repay. "He who lends [money] is greater than he who performs charity, and he who puts in capital to form a partnership with the poor is greater than all."[142]

Not only are loans a preventive form of charity, providing the needy a way to obtain the capital required to become self-sufficient—there's no shame in borrowing, and we're more inclined to lend greater amounts than we'll donate. But whether you lend or contribute, keep in mind the *Principle of Dependency:*

Do not foster dependency.

Rule of Thumb 6: The Principle of Initiatives and Endowments
Favor Initiatives over Endowments

Because we're busy, most of us desire to bestow money and be done with it. That's why we tend to support institutions rather than initiatives. Institutions tend to last longer than initiatives, and, as established entities, they seem to embody lasting prudence.

Since I've just argued that we ought not to foster dependency, you'd think I'd also say that we should contribute to endowments so institutions could become self-sustaining for the short term and independent for the long term.

That would be wise if there weren't within all organizations a dangerous dynamic that needs constantly to be resisted: over time,

nonprofit institutions tend to forget the original purpose for which they were established and focus their efforts on sustaining themselves. When that happens, they cease to serve—or to serve efficiently—the cause that initially led us to support them.

That's why, even when we channel our assistance through institutions, I believe it's better to rely on the *Principle of Initiatives and Endowments:*

Favor initiatives over endowments.

A project-oriented focus helps ensure that our contributions will be used effectively to further those values which we seek to serve, without having our assistance dissipated in serving the institution itself and elements of it or projects that are not consistent with what we seek to achieve in this world.

A century ago, philanthropist Julius Rosenwald (1862–1932) emphatically warned against a type of giving to institutions that is specifically intended to ensure their independence and longevity: endowments. In a 1913 address to the American Academy of Political and Social Science, he said, "Permanent endowment tends to lessen the amount available for immediate needs; and our immediate needs are too plain and too urgent to allow us to do the work of future generations." Further,

> I am not in sympathy with this policy of perpetuating endowments, and believe that more good can be accomplished by expending funds as trustees find opportunities for constructive work than by storing up large sums of money for long periods of time. By adopting a policy of using the Fund within this generation, we may avoid these tendencies toward bureaucracy and a formal or perfunctory attitude toward the work that almost inevitably develops in organizations that prolong their existence indefinitely. Coming generations can be relied upon to provide for their own needs as they arise.[143]

For these reasons, Rosenwald mandated that the foundation he established pay out all of its income *and* all of its principal no later than twenty-five years after his death. He argued that because it's impossible to predict the future needs of society, a dead hand shouldn't try to guide an organization through the uncharted waters of the future. This provision recognizes the likelihood that, over time, a donor's original intention will be obscured, ignored, or changed, and hence not honored. By restricting the life of his foundation, he sought to ensure that his donations were used in ways consistent with his values.[144]

I believe that in this Rosenwald is right. Our responsibility is to ensure that our wealth is used properly—a responsibility we cannot successfully delegate to those who come long after us, and over whose actions we will have little or no control.

Rule of Thumb 7: The Principle of Leverage
Contribute to Organizations That Have Leverage

As businessmen, we seek to leverage our money, time, and effort in order to yield the greatest benefit from each investment of our resources. We should approach our giving in the same way, seeking out charitable endeavors that leverage our contributions to bring the greatest effect from what we give.

Think about it this way. Society can be changed on four levels: (1) cultural, (2) political, (3) organizational, and (4) personal. Generally speaking, the greatest breadth of change happens at the cultural level, while the greatest depth of change happens at the personal level. Thus, a bestseller about raising children may broadly influence a million parents, while one parent spending time with one child can have much deeper influence on that child than any bestseller will ever have on any of its readers.

No matter which level you choose to contribute to, be sure to abide by the *Principle of Leverage* so that the effort to which you contribute is carried out in such a way that it multiplies your contribution. In other words,

*Support efforts that bring about the greatest
multiplication of results from the
time or money you contribute.*

Rule of Thumb 8: The Principle of OPM
Use Other People's Money (OPM)

In business, we obtain leverage by using other people's money (OPM) as capital, thereby providing a greater return on their funds and on ours. In supporting nonprofits, I've long thought we should seek ways to employ OPM so that the power of our own contributions will be multiplied, providing much greater assistance to an organization than would be available if we were the only contributors.

Now in business, to get others to join us in a project, we trumpet the fact that we have ourselves invested heavily in it. News of our substantial investments generally increases the amount of OPM that gets invested alongside us.

In philanthropy, however, advertising how much we've contributed often has the opposite effect. Other potential contributors may conclude that since we're already providing significant help to the cause, they don't need to do so. One way to solve this problem is to offer to match contributions that the charity raises from others. A challenge grant provides the charity incentives to work harder at raising money, and motivates givers with the fact that every dollar they contribute yields two or more for the charity.

Nonetheless, whether we raise OPM by some form of a matching grant or by other means, we've got to be sure that in courting and accepting large amounts of OPM, we don't end up diluting or even relinquishing entirely the mission of the enterprise. Where there exists a significant risk of such dilution, loans to the organization may prove a better means of assistance because they lessen the involvement in the effort by outsiders and don't require us to yield as much control as we might have to yield to other large donors.

So the *Principle of OPM* is a qualified one:

Seek OPM to fund initiatives you support,
but only so long as it can be raised without decreasing efficiency
or compromising the mission of the organization.

Sometimes I've found that I can't convince others to join me in nonprofit initiatives that I consider not only to be good, but indispensable. Early on, it looks as if the project will be expensive and that I, by my donations, may well be the only one supporting it substantially. There won't be any OPM to help support it.

In these cases, does the *Principle of OPM* require us to back away? Maybe not.

In business, when I see a company that looks like a great opportunity but everyone else seems blind to its value so that its stock languishes, I stop, take a good second look, and, if I still see value there, I buy as much of that company as I can.

In the old days, after such a purchase, I used to be disappointed when the stock went down. Then I encountered Warren Buffett's argument that such a decline in value is a reason for joy, not sorrow: it means I can purchase more of a valuable thing at an even lower price.

Buffet's argument changed my outlook in investing and it changed my way of evaluating charities that I might wind up supporting myself because I can't get OPM to help me sustain them— I now believe that if there's value in the work the charity does, then I ought to be grateful to support it, even if others don't. A good investment is a good investment, whether it reaps new wealth in the profit sector or new benefits for others in the nonprofit sector, helping to bring about the universal destination of goods.

Draw in OPM if it's prudent, but never turn your back on a charity because you're the only one who sees its importance. That charity may be given to you as an essential element in your own unique vocation: it may be the reason why you've been given your talent at wealth creation, the work that, in this life, you in particular are called to do.

Rule of Thumb 9: The Principle of Fundraising
Beware the Request to Help Raise Money

Soon after you begin to make significant contributions, you're sure to be asked to help the recipient organizations convince others to contribute to them, too. For many people that's no problem, and in fact fundraising can be a noble undertaking if they find that their spare time offers little potential for creating additional wealth.

But for those capable of creating significant additional wealth in their spare time, raising money through the traditional means employed by charitable efforts is woefully inefficient. Though charities often have a hard time accepting it, it may be better for them and more consistent with our vocation as creators of wealth for us to spend our spare time making additional money that we can then simply give to the charities.

Not getting involved in the nitty-gritty of fundraising heads off an additional problem that afflicts donors who solicit funds for charities they support: reciprocity. There's an unwritten rule that if I get you to contribute to my favorite charity, I'm obligated to support yours when you ask. The net effect is that our checks cross in the mail, the charities receive roughly the same amount of money, and you and I have wasted time calling and schmoozing each other. That's just plain inefficient, which is why I recommend you abide by the *Principle of Fundraising:*

Beware the request to help raise money.[145]

Rule of Thumb 10: The Principle of Focus
Stay Focused on a Few Initiatives

We put blinders on horses to prevent them from going astray. Blinders limit their distractions and keep them focused on the course ahead. That way, they're more likely to reach their destination sooner and in the most direct fashion possible.

Especially in philanthropy, with many needy and worthy organizations and persons vying for your attention, it's hard to stay fo-

*"I do ballet, conservation, starvation, cancer research,
the needy, a little art, and a smidgen of Farmington."*

cused. Before long, you can find yourself involved in so many projects that you're not really serving any of them well, and even your financial contributions are not being used effectively. That's why it's essential that you rely on the *Principle of Focus*, which mandates that you

*Stay focused on a few initiatives
rather than getting involved in many.*

Don't dilute the effectiveness of your contributions or even squander them by failing to employ due diligence in choosing organizations and by failing to regulate your involvement in them by the Ten Rules of Thumb we've considered here. By relying on these principles, your philanthropic efforts will not only be incrementally better, there will be a quantum improvement in the results you achieve.

◆ ◆ ◆

For convenience sake, here's a list of all ten of the Rules of Thumb.

The Ten Rules of Thumb for Donors

1. Support indispensable causes to which your support is indispensable
2. Seek synergy
3. Know who's in control
4. Consider the pros and cons of anonymity
5. Do not foster dependency
6. Favor initiatives over endowments
7. Contribute to organizations with leverage
8. Use other people's money (OPM)
9. Beware the request to help raise money
10. Stay focused on a few initiatives

questions to ask

To help me abide by the Ten Rules of Thumb in my choices for charitable contributions, I ask (and answer for myself) strategic questions about an organization before I contribute to it or get involved with it in other ways. Essentially, these questions are just another way of ensuring that I've taken a good look at the organization and know what I'm getting involved in and what my involvement will be. You may find them helpful for the same purpose.

Is the group or cause explicit, internally, about its philosophy and goals?

Do you agree with its philosophy and goals?

Do you agree with its methods?

Is it engaged in highly leveraged activities?

Does it have the potential to create either a great breadth of change (such as a renewal in all of society) or a great depth of change (such as long-lasting, fundamental transformations of individuals)?

Will your contribution be the tipping point, making the difference between the failure or success of the effort?

Is someone else or some other group already performing essentially the same task with at least moderate effectiveness, keeping in mind the *Rule of Indispensability*?

Are you being entrepreneurial in your approach, helping start efforts which otherwise have not attracted other support, and then withdrawing your assistance as they gain strength and are able to appeal to others for support?

Do you bring any particular knowledge, expertise, or ability to the project, or can you engage others to realize your objectives, freeing you for other efforts where you are truly indispensable?

Is a capable person in charge of the effort?

Does the degree to which you will be permitted to monitor, participate in, or control the effort correspond positively to the degree of support that you are providing to it?

What percentage of support do your contributions comprise, and are you happy with that percentage?

Are there other potential future funding sources for this effort?

Will your support encourage others to give?

Should you use a challenge grant?

Is the money going for an endowment?

Is a contribution understandably expected from you because of your membership or other relationship to the organization?

Is there a strategic plan with goals that are shared by board and staff?

Are the plans well conceived and likely to work out as proposed?

Is the organization led by competent and visionary individuals?

What would happen if the founder or current chief executive departed?

Are accounting and financial record-keeping systems in place?

Do you have access to the financial records?

Can the effort serve as a model that can be replicated elsewhere?

I previously noted that in philanthropy we must be prudent, but never hard. These questions and the Ten Rules of Thumb can help you be prudent, but remember that they're no more than guidelines, to which there are always exceptions.

Use them to help you grow more experienced in giving; don't let them become an excuse for not giving at all. May they increase your generosity and your wisdom, and bring you the joy that comes from discovering the meaning of your money and living in accord with it!

endnotes

[1] Floyd Arthur Harper (1905–1973). "The Greatest Economic Charity" (from Mary Sennholtz, ed., *On Freedom and Free Enterprise*, 1956).

[2] Shakespeare (1564–1616). *King John*, II, I, 587.

[3] "I tell you that it is the greatest good for a human being to have discussions every day about virtue and the other things you hear me talking about, examining myself and others, and that the unexamined life is not livable for a human being." Socrates (469–399 B.C.) quoted in Plato, *Apology*, sect. 38.

[4] Tacitus (c. 55–c. 117). *Annals*, XIII, 55.

[5] For the sake of convenience, we'll call these things the *fundamentals*, and later, in Chapter 3, will define precisely the kinds of things that are included in them, and the kinds of things that are not.

[6] Alan Guth (b. 1947), quoted in Chapter 8 of Stephen Hawking's *A Brief History of Time*. In this quote, Guth is remarking on the fact that, in the judgment of modern physics, about 13.7 billion years ago our entire universe sprang into existence from nothing. According to modern astrophysics, literally everything that is has been given to us for free.

[7] John Stuart Mill (1806–1873). *Principles of Political Economy*, Bk II, II, 6.

[8] Germain Grisez (b. 1929). *Living a Christian Life* (Franciscan Press, 1993), 790. The Catholic Church has made this understanding of the goods of the earth a central part of its social teachings. See *Gaudium et spes*, 69; John Paul II, *Christifideles laici*, 43.

[9] Grisez also notes that "This principle does not mean that in the beginning human persons jointly *owned* the material world, with each

having an equal share: no such primitive social order ever existed. Therefore, the universal destination of goods does not imply even a basic or prima facie claim on the part of each individual to an equal portion of the world's good" (*Living a Christian Life*, 790).

10 Although I think that the term "universal destination of goods" serves well to indicate this unique quality of the goods of the earth, I will, for the sake of readability, sometimes substitute for it the term "common good." In those instances, I mean no more by the term "common good" (and no less) than what is meant by "the universal destination of goods."

11 Matthew 19:21–25.

12 Aristotle, *Politics*, Bk. 2, Part 5.

13 Cicero, *De Officiis*, I, 7.

14 Aquinas, *Summa Theologica*, II, II, 66.

15 Aristotle, *Politics*, 1263b. Also, in that same passage: "No one, when men have all things in common, will any longer set an example of liberality or do any liberal action; for liberality consists in the use which is made of property."

16 J. Paul Getty (1892–1976), quoted in *Observer* (London, Nov. 3, 1957).

17 Gerald Brenan (1894–1987). *Thoughts in a Dry Season* (1978).

18 1 Timothy 6:10.

19 Mark Twain (1835–1910). "More Maxims of Mark" (from *Mark Twain: Collected Tales, Sketches, Speeches, & Essays, 1891–1910*, Library of America, 1992).

20 John Updike (b. 1932). Piet Hanema in *Couples* (1968).

21 Although I have not directly adopted the terms and distinctions proposed by Germain Grisez in his eminently lucid discussion of wealth and poverty, I am heavily indebted to Grisez for the inspiration behind many of the distinctions I make in this section. For a less personal, more theoretical discussion of many of the themes touched on here, see *Living a Christian Life*, 753–834: "Work, Subhuman Realities, and Property."

22 Samuel Johnson (1709–1784). Letter to James Boswell (June 3, 1782).

23 James Baldwin (1924–1987). "Fifth Avenue, Uptown: a letter from Harlem" (from *Nobody Knows My Name*, 1961).

24 Recall (and continue to remember as we proceed through this discussion) the point I made a few pages ago: in this chapter, our question here is restricted to how much money is enough; later we'll consider

whether there are expenditures beyond *bare necessities* and *genuine needs* that would be right and good even for those who cannot afford to pay for all of their *bare necessities* and *genuine needs.*

[25] Ralph Waldo Emerson (1803–1882). "Wealth" (from *The Conduct of Life*, 1860).

[26] Mary Quant (b. 1936). Quoted in *Observer* (London, Nov. 2, 1986).

[27] Marcus Aurelius (121–180). *Meditations*, VIII, 33.

[28] Emerson, "Wealth."

[29] Ibid.

[30] Samuel Johnson. Quoted in Boswell's *Life of Johnson* (July 20, 1763).

[31] Horace (65–8 B.C.). *Odes*, IV, 9, l. 45.

[32] Winston Churchill (1874–1965).

[33] In Chapter 11 we'll consider ways that even very wealthy folks can actually use their non-essential wealth to do just this for their children.

[34] Mark 12:41–44.

[35] Lawana Blackwell (b. 1952). *The Courtship of the Vicar's Daughter* (1998). Her exact words were, "He had learned over the years that poor people did not feel so poor when allowed to give occasionally."

[36] Plato (427 B.C.–347 B.C.). *The Republic, Book IV.*

[37] John Dryden (1631–1700). "Absalom and Achitophel" (1681), pt. I, 1, 559. Line 2 means that "only those things that deserved reward failed to be rewarded."

[38] Emerson, "Wealth."

[39] George Bernard Shaw (1856–1950). Preface to *Major Barbara* (1905).

[40] Tacitus (c. 55–c. 117). *Annals*, 6.

[41] Helen Keller (1880–1968).

[42] Emerson. "Manners," from *Essays, Second Series* (1844).

[43] In "The Wife of Bath's Tale" in his *Canterbury Tales.*

[44] David Elkind (b. 1931). *Miseducation* (1987).

[45] Gertrude Stein (1874–1946). *Wars I Have Seen* (1945).

[46] F. Scott Fitzgerald (1896–1940). From "The Rich Boy" in *All the Sad Young Men* (1926). In his short story "The Snows of Kilimanjaro," Ernest Hemingway (1899–1961) responded to Fitzgerald's assertion that the rich are different from you and me: "Yes, they have more money."

[47] Alexander Pope (1688–1744). *Thoughts on Various Subjects.*

[48] Agnes E. Meyer (1887–1970). *Out of These Roots* (1953).

49 George Bernard Shaw (1856–1950). Boss Mangan, in *Heartbreak House,* act 2.

50 Seneca (3 B.C.–A.D. 65).

51 Muriel Beadle (b. 1915). *Where Has All the Ivy Gone?* (1972).

52 Hillaire Belloc (1870–1953). "Fatigued" (1923).

53 Spike Milligan (1918–2002). *Puckoon,* 1963.

54 Josh Billings, pseud. of Henry Wheeler Shaw (1818–1885).

55 W. H. Auden (1907–73). "Postscript: The Almighty Dollar" in *The Dyer's Hand* (1962). A rentier is a landlord.

56 Emerson, "Wealth."

57 Arthur Hugh Clough (1819–1861). "Dipsychus" (l. 1–6).

58 Woody Allen (b. 1935). "The Early Essays" in *Without Feathers* (1976).

59 Edgar Watson Howe (1853–1937).

60 Thomas Aquinas (c. 1225–74). *Summa Theologica,* II–II, 188, 7.

61 Emerson, "Wealth."

62 Barry Schwartz (b. 1946) develops this theme ably in his recent book, *The Paradox of Choice.*

63 Jean Kerr (b. 1923). From "Poor Richard," act 1.

64 Larry McMurtry (b. 1936). Danny Deck, in *Some Can Whistle.*

65 Seneca (c. 4 B.C.–A.D. 65). *Letters to Lucius,* 16.

66 John Ruskin (1819–1900). *The Eagle's Nest* (1872).

67 John D. Rockefeller (1839–1937). "The Difficult Art of Giving" (1907).

68 Philip Larkin (1922–1986). From his poem "Money."

69 Maimonides (1135–1204). "On the Evils" (From *Guide for the Perplexed,* 1190).

70 Emerson, "Wealth."

71 Ibid.

72 Henry Fielding (1707–1754). Mariana, in *The Miser,* act 3, sc. 7.

73 Samuel Johnson (1709–1784). Quoted in Boswell's *Life of Johnson.* Vol. VI, Chap. IX.

74 Chinese proverb.

75 David Hume (1711–1776). "On Money," in *Essays Moral, Political, and Literary,* Part II.

76 Emerson, "Wealth."

77 Sylvia Porter (1913–1991). *Sylvia Porter's Money Book,* Chap. 1.

78 Donald Trump (b. 1946). *Trump: Art of the Deal.*

79 Mason Cooley (b. 1927). *City Aphorisms.*

[80] Indeed, when it's feasible, it may be better to rent things rather than own them, so as to avoid the troubles and responsibilities that accompany many possessions.

[81] John Ruskin (1819–1900). *Unto this Land*, IV, 77.

[82] This is what John Stuart Mill meant when he said that "When private property in land is not expedient, it is unjust." Mill, *Principles of Political Economy*, Bk. II, II, 6.

[83] Sophie Tucker (1884–1966).

[84] Aquinas, *Summa Theologica* II–II, 66, 7. Aquinas is quoting St. Ambrose (c. 333–397) from Ambrose's *Decretals* (*Dist.* xlvii, *can. Sicut* ii).

[85] Matthew 19:21–25.

[86] Tiruvalluvar (c. 5th century A.D.). From the *Sacred Kural*, vs. IV. 2.

[87] For a full discussion of this topic, see Germaine Grisez and Russell Shaw, *Personal Vocation* (2003).

[88] Matthew 19:21–25.

[89] John D. Rockefeller, "The Difficult Art of Giving" (1907), in *America's Voluntary Spirit: A Book of Readings* (1983).

[90] William Henry Boetcker (1873–1962). From "Ten Cannots."

[91] Samuel Johnson (1709–1784). Quoted in James Boswell, *Life of Samuel Johnson*, May 1776 (1791).

[92] Rockefeller, "The Difficult Art of Giving." (1907).

[93] Richard Wilbur (b. 1921). Quoted from "Junk."

[94] Maimonides (1135–1204).

[95] For this theme and for a number of others in these pages, I am indebted to members of the Acton Institute and in particular to the senior researcher there, and in particular to Father Robert Sirico and Samuel Gregg.

[96] Aristotle, *Rhetoric*, 1361a.

[97] Matthew 25:14.

[98] Hillaire Belloc (1870–1953). "Lord Finchley," in *More Peers* (1911).

[99] John D. Rockefeller (1839–1937), from a 1905 interview quoted in Peter Collier and David Horowitz, *The Rockefellers, an American Dynasty* (1976), 48.

[100] Vida D. Scudder (1861–1954).

[101] Margaret C. Anderson (1886–1973). *My Thirty Years' War* (1930).

102 St. Basil the Great (329–379). From his *Hom. in Luc. xii, 18,* quoted in Aquinas, *Summa Theologica,* II, II, q. 66, 2, reply to objection 2.

103 Emerson, "Wealth."

104 Andrew Carnegie (1835–1919). From "Wealth," an essay that is popularly known these days as "The Gospel of Wealth" because of a phrase Carnegie employed in the essay.

105 Francis Bacon (1561–1626). *Of Expense* (1612).

106 Irving Berlin (1888–1989).

107 Oliver Goldsmith (1730–1774). "The Deserted Village" (l. 51–52).

108 See Chapter 12.

109 Julius Rosenwald (1862–1932). Quoted in *Wealthy and Wise,* 164.

110 Rosenberg, *Wealthy and Wise,* 165.

111 See page 19: *Ownership is the prudential division of property into yours and mine.*

112 John Kenneth Galbraith (b. 1908) remarks how lack of this very motive affects the efficiency of government: "You will find that the State is the kind of organization which, though it does big things badly, does small things badly, too."

113 Ronald Reagan (1911–2004). Televised address, October 27, 1964. "A Time for Choosing," published in *Speaking My Mind* (1989).

114 Lucy Larcom (1824–1893). *A New England Girlhood* (1889).

115 Rockefeller, "The Difficult Art of Giving."

116 Sir Thomas Browne (1605–1682).

117 Aquinas, *Summa Theologica,* II–II, 188, 7.

118 Psalm 41: 1.

119 See Chapter 4.

120 James Russell Lowell (1819–1891). *Among my Books.* 1st Series.

121 Proverbs 22:29.

122 Robert Menzies (1894–1978). Quoted in *Wit and Wisdom of Robert Menzies* (1982).

123 Cicero (106 B.C.–43 B.C.). *De Officiis,* I, 20.

124 Like many of the other human traits we've considered in these pages, this temptation is not new. Writing more than two thousand years ago, Aristotle (384–322 B.C.) bemoaned this failing in men he knew: "Some persons are led to believe that . . . the whole idea of their lives is that they ought either to increase their money without limit, or at any rate, not to lose it. The origin of this disposition in men is that

they are intent upon living only, and not upon living well; and, as their desires are unlimited, they also desire that the means of gratifying them should be without limit" *Politics* (1258a).

[125] Margaret Thatcher (b. 1925). Quoted in *Times* (London, Jan. 12, 1986).

[126] 2 Chronicles 31:5–6: "As soon as the command was spread abroad, the people of Israel gave in abundance the first fruits of grain, wine, oil, honey, and of all the produce of the field; and they brought in abundantly the tithe of everything. And the people of Israel and Judah who lived in the cities of Judah also brought in the tithe of cattle and sheep, and they dedicated things which had been consecrated to the Lord their God, and laid them in heaps."

[127] Samuel Johnson (1709–1784). Quoted in Boswell's *Life of Johnson* (April 17, 1778).

[128] Evelyn Waugh (1903–66) claimed that "Money is only useful when you get rid of it. It is like the odd card in 'Old Maid'; the player who is finally left with it has lost."

[129] St. Augustine (354–430). *City of God*, V, 18.

[130] Harriot K. Hunt (1805–1875). *Glances and Glimpses* (1856).

[131] Quoted by Emerson in "Wealth."

[132] There's a basic introduction to them in Chapter 10 (131–167) of *Inspired Philanthropy*, which is entitled *The Many Ways to Give.*

[133] For more on the virtues of family involvement in philanthropy, see *Estate Planning for the Healthy Wealthy Family*, 120–123.

[134] Goethe (1749–1832), quoted by Emerson in "Wealth."

[135] Barbara Ehrenreich (b. 1941). "Oh, Those Family Values," from *The Snarling Citizen* (1995).

[136] Ecclesiastes 5:12.

[137] George M. Humphrey (1890–1970). *Look* (Feb. 23, 1954).

[138] Page 114: Money Increases the interdependence of humans.

[139] 1 Corinthians 13:3–4.

[140] Carnegie, "Wealth" (1889).

[141] *Babylonian Talmud: Hagigah 5a*, quoted in David G. Dalin, "Judaism's War on Poverty," in *Policy Review* (Sept./Oct. 1997).

[142] *Babylonian Talmud: Tractate Shabbath*, Folio 63a, quoted in David G. Dalin, "Judaism's War on Poverty," in *Policy Review* (Sept./Oct. 1997).

[143] Julius Rosenwald (1862–1932). Quoted in "Debates on Perpetuity," an article by Martin Morse Wooster in the July/August 1998 issue of *Philanthropy.*

144 Rosenwald, "Principles of Public Giving," *Atlantic Monthly*, May 1929. Anthologized in America's Voluntary Spirit, Brian O'Connell, ed. (Foundation Center, NY, 1983), 119–128).

145 Here, as generally involve reciprocity, and such a solicitation might be appropriate. Lending your name, but not giving time, to a charity may help that organization raise funds without impairing your own ability to give them more in an outright donation by earning more in your vocation. Likewise, offering a matching donation may help, but surely should not be ruled out.

index

about the author

Frank J. Hanna, CEO of Hanna Capital, has started and financed a number of successful businesses, has also become a philanthropist, and has been awarded for his thinking and his giving with the William B. Simon Prize for Philanthropic Leadership and the David R. Jones Award for Philanthropy. He has been highly involved in promoting educational liberty for the last 25 years, helping to start three Catholic schools in Atlanta, leading various efforts for school reform, and chairing the President's Advisory Commission on Educational Excellence for Hispanic Americans. Mr. Hanna is the founder of the Solidarity Association, which among other efforts, recently obtained the oldest extant copy of portions of the Gospels of Luke and John, which were then given to the Vatican. He lives in Atlanta, Georgia.